I0797805

ATLAS of HORSES AND PONIES

For Lady, Willow and Rusty, who I've never forgotten.
And with special thanks to John for teaching me so much about horses.
F. E.

Author: Frances Evans
Illustrator: Adrienne Green
Publishing Director: Piers Pickard
Publisher: Rebecca Hunt
Editorial Director: Joe Fullman
Art Director: Andy Mansfield
Commissioning Editor: Kate Baker
Consultant: Camilla de la Bedoyere
Print Production: Nigel Longuet

Published in October 2025
by Lonely Planet Global Limited
CRN: 554153
ISBN: 978-1-83758-670-7
10 9 8 7 6 5 4 3 2

Printed in Malaysia

All rights reserved. No part of this publication may be reproduced, stored in a retrieval system or transmitted in any form by any means, electronic, mechanical, photocopying, recording, or otherwise except brief extracts for the purpose of review, without the written permission of the publisher. Lonely Planet and the Lonely Planet logo are trademarks of Lonely Planet and are registered in the US Patent and Trademark Office and in other countries.

Although the author and Lonely Planet have taken all reasonable care in preparing this book, we make no warranty about the accuracy or completeness of its content and, to the maximum extent permitted, disclaim all liability from its use.

Stay in Touch
Lonelyplanet.com/contact

Lonely Planet Office:
IRELAND
Digital Depot, Roe Lane (off Thomas St.), Digital Hub, Dublin 8, D08 TCV4, Ireland

Paper in this book is certified against the Forest Stewardship Council™ standards. FSC™ promotes environmentally responsible, socially beneficial and economically viable management of the world's forests.

lonely planet KIDS

ATLAS of HORSES AND PONIES

illustrated by
Adrienne Green

written by
Frances Evans

CONTENTS

A WORLD OF HORSES AND PONIES

Welcome to the wonderful world of horses and ponies! From the fabulous Friesian and dainty Falabella to the dashing Arab and tough Exmoor, this book will take you on an a-neigh-zing journey around the planet to meet over 100 beautiful breeds. Some are horses you might encounter at your local riding stables, while others may be less familiar.

HOW THIS BOOK WORKS

You'll find a map at the start of each chapter so you can see where the horses and ponies come from, while the profile pages give you the lowdown on each breed, their characteristics, and care needs. There are also special entries that explore topics such as cute foals, horsey sports, donkeys and mules, mythical horses, and much more!

It is estimated that there are around 60 million wild and domestic horses in the world today.

WHAT IS A HORSE? AND WHAT IS A PONY?

Horses are hoofed, plant-eating mammals, known for their agility, speed, and strength. We're not certain exactly when horses were first tamed (or "domesticated") by humans, but it may have been in around 4000 BCE in Central Asia. They quickly became some of our most loyal and important animal friends, helping us to farm, travel, and build civilizations, carrying us into battles, and providing comfort and companionship.

Horses and ponies belong to the same species—*Equus caballus* (or the domestic horse). The main differences between horses and ponies are their shape and size. A horse has a slender build and is usually considered to be over 14.2 hands high. Ponies are smaller than this and have sturdy, stocky bodies. Some breeds, such as the Falabella and Icelandic, fall into the "Pony" category in this book (see page 9) because they are smaller than 14.2 hands high, but they are often called small horses rather than ponies because they have the same proportions as a bigger horse, just in a little form.

WHAT IS A BREED?

A group of horses that has been deliberately bred to have the same characteristics is known as a breed. Different breeds have been developed all over the world for different jobs and purposes, and they often reflect the environment that they come from.

For example, the mighty Clydesdale (1) was bred to work on Scottish farms, the dazzling Akhal-Teke (2) emerged from the deserts of Turkmenistan, and the tiny but tough Spiti (3) was developed to trek through the icy Himalayan Mountains. You can think of all the breeds you meet in this book as equine ambassadors for their home nations and cultures.

HOW CAN I MEET HORSES?

Owning a horse or pony is a dream goal for many people. But it is an enormous responsibility and a long-term commitment—a well-cared-for horse can live for 25 years or more, while many ponies live beyond 30 years. Horses and ponies need daily care, lots of space, and other horsey friends to live a happy and healthy life.

There are plenty of ways to be around horses and ponies without owning one. The best place to start is your local riding center. Here, you can learn about basic horse care and how to handle and ride a horse. You could also visit a sanctuary or rehoming center to meet horses and ponies, and support the welfare of these beautiful animals.

ATLAS OF A HORSE

Whether they're a mighty Shire or a sturdy Shetland, all horses and ponies share the same basic features. Here's some essential horse geography.

BACK

The back is where the saddle goes when you ride a horse. It's important to know where a horse's back starts and ends so you can put your saddle in the right place—if a saddle sits too far forward (on the withers) or too far back (on the loin), this could be uncomfortable for a horse.

MANE AND FORELOCK

The long hair on the top of a horse's neck is called its mane. It protects the horse from the weather and biting insects. The piece of mane that falls between the horse's ears is called its forelock.

TAIL

A horse uses its tail for balance, to express how it's feeling, and for swatting away flies.

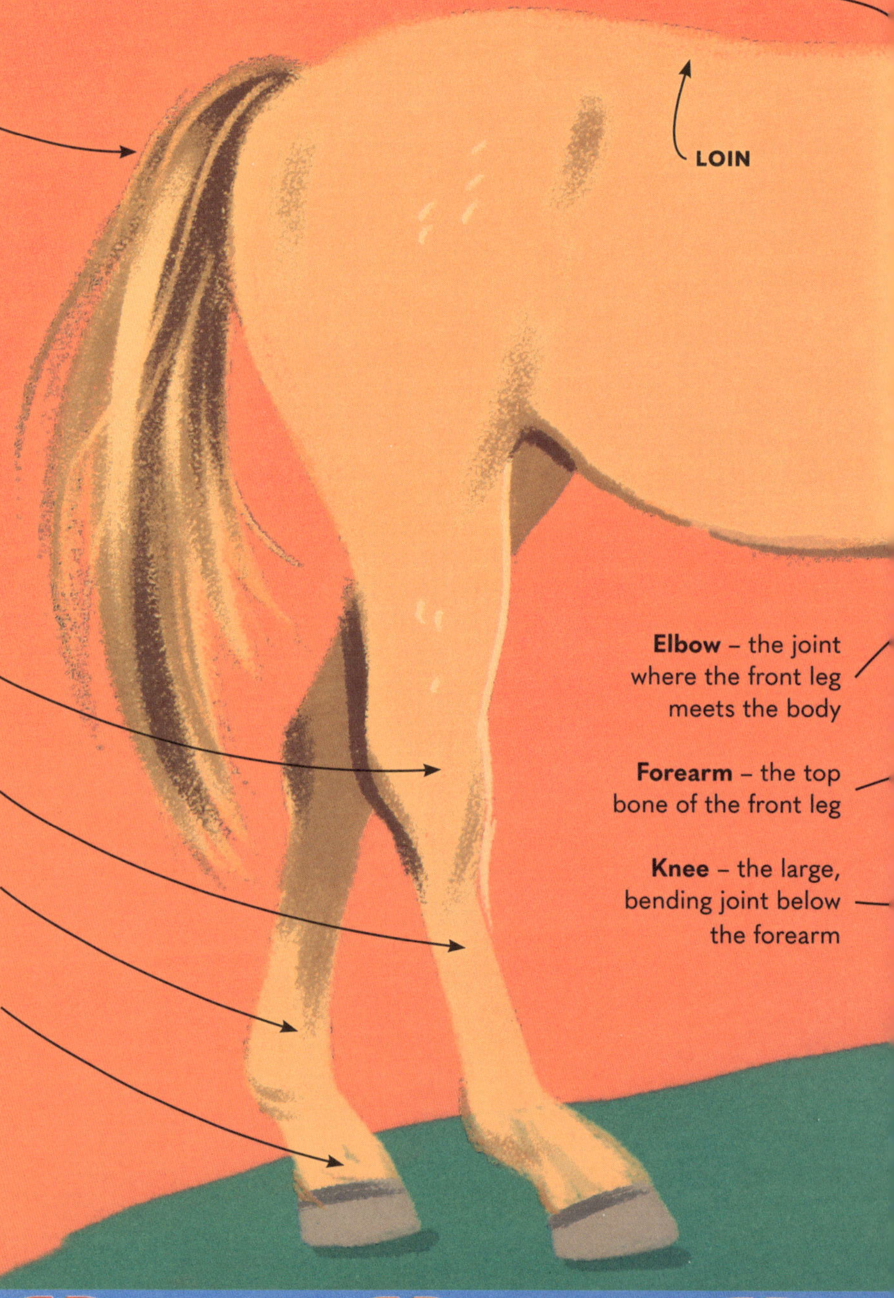

LOIN

LEGS

A horse's front and back legs are made up of several sections:

Hock – the large joint on the back legs, located in a similar spot to the knee on the front legs

Cannon – the lower bone of a horse's leg

Fetlock – a joint that connects the cannon bone to the pastern

Pastern– the part of the leg between the fetlock and hoof, which allows the hoof to flex and cushions the impact of each step

Elbow – the joint where the front leg meets the body

Forearm – the top bone of the front leg

Knee – the large, bending joint below the forearm

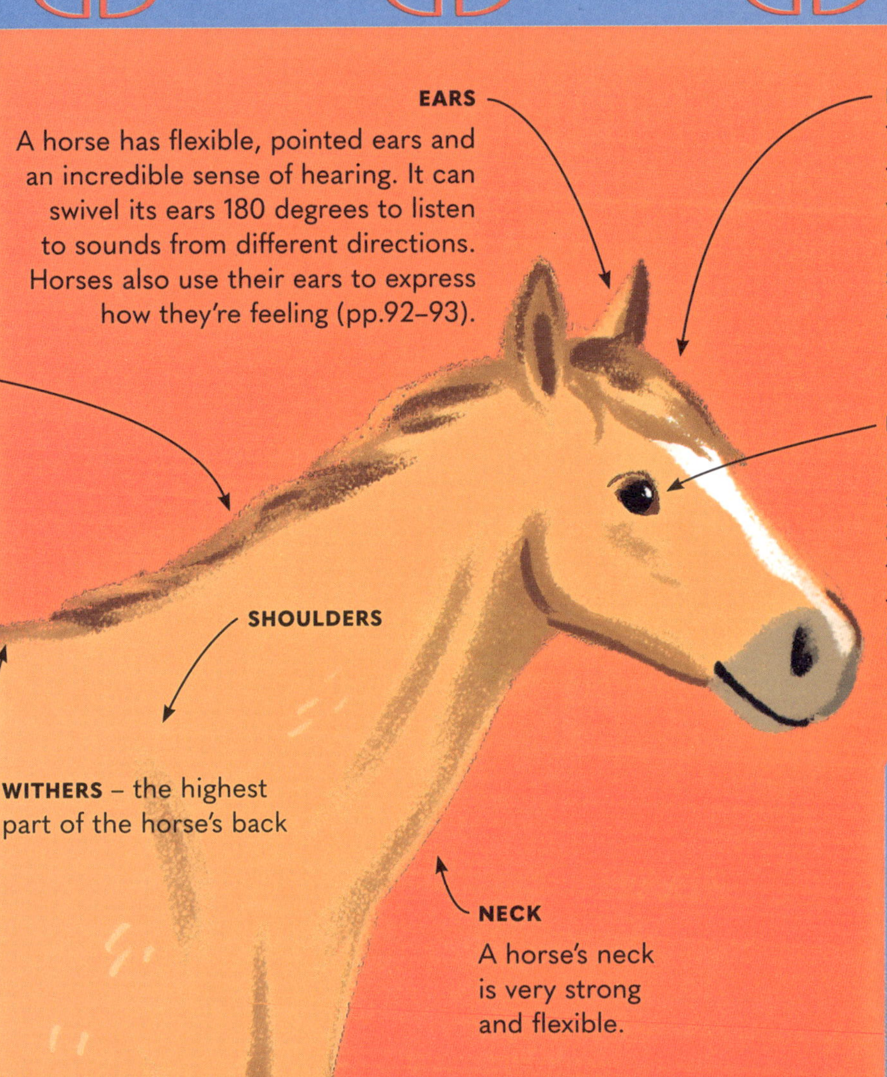

EARS

A horse has flexible, pointed ears and an incredible sense of hearing. It can swivel its ears 180 degrees to listen to sounds from different directions. Horses also use their ears to express how they're feeling (pp.92–93).

HEAD

The nose, mouth, and chin are called the muzzle. It is very soft and covered in whiskers that help the horse sense things close to its face. Horses use their strong sense of smell to communicate with one another and interpret their surroundings.

EYES

Horses have very big eyes that sit on each side of their head, so they can see nearly 360 degrees around. In the wild, this allows them to look out for predators without having to turn their head. They can't see immediately in front or behind them, however.

SHOULDERS

WITHERS – the highest part of the horse's back

NECK

A horse's neck is very strong and flexible.

HOOF

The hoof (foot) has a soft interior and a hard exterior. The outside of the hoof is made up of a strong material called keratin—the same material that forms your fingernails.

Horses are extremely sensitive to touch. A rider will apply a different pressure to the reins or change the position of their body in the saddle to tell a horse how they want them to move.

MEASURING HORSES

A horse's height is measured from its **withers** to the ground using a unit of measurement called a hand. One hand is equal to 4 inches (10.2 cm).

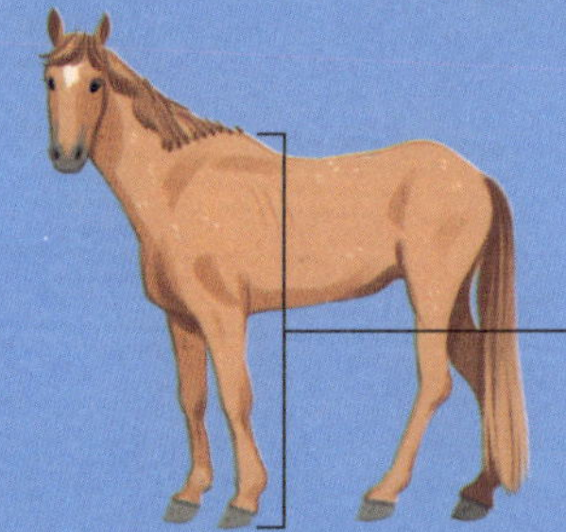

HORSE TYPES

Horses can be grouped into three basic types. In this book, each breed's type is listed in its profile box:

See glossary on p.110 for more information.

COLORS AND MARKINGS

Domestic horses and ponies have an incredible range of colors and markings —from glossy chestnut and stylish black to sleek gray and even spots! Some breeds are deliberately bred to have (or not have) particular colors and markings. Here's a guide to some key color terms.

CHESTNUT

Chestnut horses have red-brown coats, manes, and tails. They may have white markings on their face and legs, but they never have any black hair.

BAY

A bay horse has a rich brown coat with a black mane, tail, and legs. Bay ranges from very dark brown (almost black) to a brighter red-brown color.

DUN

A dun horse has a tan coat with a darker mane, tail, and legs. Dun horses also have a dark stripe (called a dorsal stripe) on their back and stripe markings (called zebra stripes) on their legs.

ROAN

A roan horse has a mix of white and dark hairs, which gives its coat a stunning, shimmery look. For example, a black roan horse has black hairs mixed with white, while a red roan has chestnut hairs mixed with white.

FACE AND LEG MARKINGS

Horses and ponies have unique markings on their legs and face, which are often used as a way of telling individuals apart. Here are some common markings to look for. These markings can appear on their own or in combinations.

FACE MARKINGS

STAR | SNIP | STRIP (OR STRIPE) | BLAZE | BALD | ERMINE

SPOTTED

A spotted horse is unmistakable! This striking pattern is sometimes known as appaloosa. Appaloosa is also the name of an American breed with a spotty coat (p.22).

BLACK

Black is a rare coat color for horses as it is caused by a special gene. Some horse breeds have been deliberately bred to be all-black, such as the Friesian (p.49).

GRAY

Gray horses have white hair and black skin. They are born with a brown or black coat that becomes paler as they grow up until, later in adulthood, they are gray or completely white. Most horses that look "white" are actually gray. True white horses (horses that have pink skin and are born with white hair) are very rare.

Gray horses with spots of lighter gray or white on their coats are called dapple-gray.

PINTO

Pinto (also called paint or colored) horses have coats made up of patches of white and another color. Different color combinations have different names. For example, a horse with black and white patches is called piebald, while a horse with patches of white and any color other than black is skewbald.

PALOMINO AND BUCKSKIN

Palomino horses have golden coats and white manes and tails. Some palomino horses have blue eyes. Horses with golden coats and dark manes and tails are called buckskins.

LEG MARKINGS

The leg markings on a horse have different names, which reflect how much of the leg is covered.

CARING FOR A HORSE OR PONY

Caring for a horse or pony is lots of fun, but it is also a big responsibility. Here's a guide to the basics, so you can make sure any horse or pony you look after lives a happy and healthy life.

FOOD

Fresh grass is a horse's natural food. When that isn't available, dried grass (called hay) is the next best thing. Horses must always have access to fresh water to stay healthy. In hot weather, horses should also be given a salt block to lick, as they lose lots of salt from their body when they sweat.

Horses have small stomachs and need to eat little and often—in the wild, a horse will graze for about 18 hours a day. It's important to make sure your horse or pony is eating the right amount of food—too little can cause them to lose weight and too much can make them overweight and lead to health problems.

Horses can be fed small amounts of oats, barley, and corn for extra nutrition in colder months, when there isn't as much fresh grass around. They can also be fed occasional vegetable and fruit treats, such as carrots.

COMPANY AND OUTSIDE SPACE

Horses are herd animals and enjoy being outside with other horses and ponies. As well as providing companionship, it's important to give your horse as much space to move around in as possible. You could introduce fun activities to your horse's field, too. For example, some horses enjoy kicking a ball when they're feeling playful.

Before a horse or pony is let out into a field, the area must be checked to ensure it is free from toxic plants. A plant called ragwort is especially poisonous to horses and ponies.

SHELTER

Horses that live outdoors should always have access to a shelter, so they can escape from bad weather or flies. The shelter should be built on well-drained ground, out of the wind, and have an entrance large enough to let all the horses in the field come and go freely.

Some horses, especially valuable sport horses, are housed in stables. This makes feeding, grooming, and health checks easier. But horses are social animals and can get lonely if they are kept alone. Many pet horses are let out into a field with other horses during the day and taken into an individual stable at night, so they get the best of both worlds.

GROOMING

Most horses and ponies love being groomed (having their coat brushed). This is a great way to build a bond with a horse, and it helps keep the animal's coat and skin healthy. They should be groomed each day, and before and after every riding session. As well as pampering your horsey pal, this is a good opportunity to check for injuries or signs of illness.

HOOVES AND TEETH

Like your fingernails, a horse's hooves are always growing. If you have a horse or pony, you will need to check its hooves and pick out any mud each day. Hooves must also be regularly trimmed by a farrier (someone who specializes in hoof care).

Some horses, especially working horses or sport horses, wear metal or plastic shoes as extra protection. A farrier will check and refit a horse's shoes every eight weeks or so to make sure the feet are in good condition and the shoes are comfortable.

Like its hooves, a horse's teeth grow constantly. Horses and ponies should be checked by a horsey dentist every six months, to make sure their teeth are a healthy length.

NORTH AMERICA

The land of ranches, rodeos, and cowboys, North America loves its horses. All modern North American breeds are descended from horses that were brought to the continent by European settlers from the 1500s onward. Many of these breeds had important roles to play—they are horses that carried pioneers over inhospitable mountains, took soldiers into battle during the Civil War, and rounded up cattle on the Great Plains. Others, like the Appaloosa, were developed by North America's Indigenous peoples and reflect another side of the continent's story.

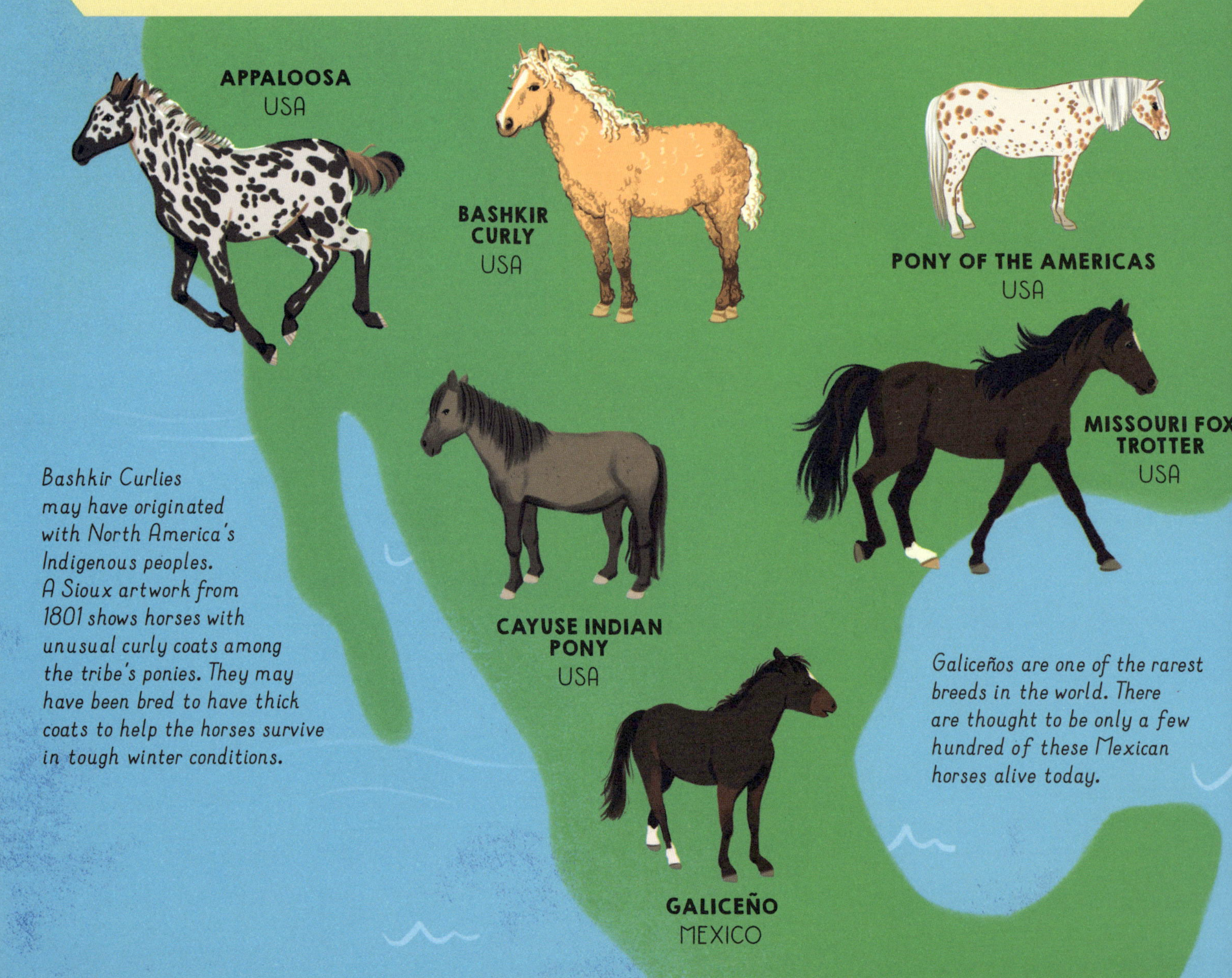

Bashkir Curlies may have originated with North America's Indigenous peoples. A Sioux artwork from 1801 shows horses with unusual curly coats among the tribe's ponies. They may have been bred to have thick coats to help the horses survive in tough winter conditions.

Galiceños are one of the rarest breeds in the world. There are thought to be only a few hundred of these Mexican horses alive today.

A horse called Beautiful Jim Key was a famous performer in America in the early 20th century. Described as the "smartest horse in the world," Jim was said to be able to count, spell, and tell the time.

INDIGENOUS PEOPLES AND HORSES

North America is probably the original home of the horse —it evolved there about 56 million years ago, then spread into Europe and Asia. But all horses in North America mysteriously died out about 10,000 years ago. Native Americans first encountered horses in the 16th century, when European colonizers (and their horses) arrived. At first, they were afraid of these animals because European settlers rode on horseback to capture villages. But as herds began to roam free, they were adopted by Indigenous peoples, helping them to hunt, travel, trade, and protect their land from European invaders. Horses became an important part of Indigenous culture, celebrated in art and dances, and loved as companions.

CANADIAN HORSE

The Canadian Horse (or Cheval Canadien) is a rare and beautiful breed. All Canadian Horses can be traced back to a group of mares and stallions that were sent from France to eastern Canada between 1665 and 1670. These horses had been hand-picked from the royal stables of the king of France, Louis XIV, and they were probably a mix of Bretons (p.53) and Norman Cobs (p.50).

Once the horses set hoof in Canada, they were rented out to French settlers who were farming the mountainous landscape in what is now the province of Quebec. Over the next hundred years, the horses were bred in isolation, developing a unique look and personality.

These hardy horses were bred to cope with Canada's long, cold winters. Their strength and sturdiness made them ideal for pulling sleighs.

HORSE PROFILE

Country: Canada **Type:** Light
Height: 14–16.2 hands
Colors: Usually black, bay, or brown, but can be any color
Personality: Loyal, robust, intelligent

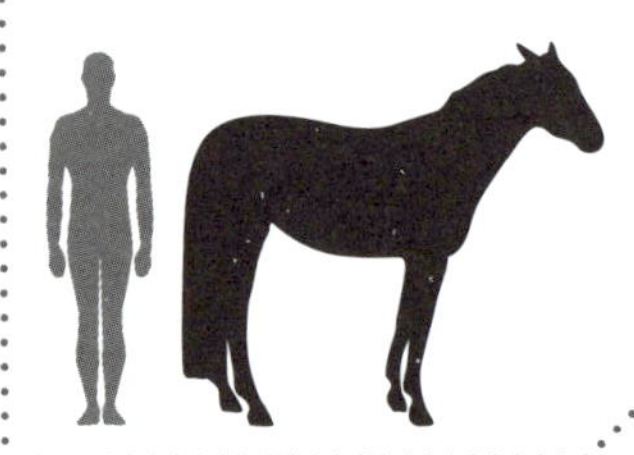

Nicknamed the "little iron horse," this compact, strong breed was used for a range of jobs, such as pulling sleighs and stagecoaches, racing, farmwork, and carrying soldiers into battle during the American Civil War. In 2002, they were made an official symbol of Canada, which shows thier importance in the nation's history and culture.

MORGAN

The Morgan originated in the US state of Vermont in the 1790s and was one of the first breeds to be developed in America. All Morgans are descended from a stallion named Figure, who was owned by a man called Justin Morgan. Figure was a small horse, but was an exceptionally fast racer and hard worker. Figure was bred with local mares and passed on his strength, stamina, and gentle nature to his foals.

In the 19th century, Morgans were seen as perfect all-purpose horses. They were used for riding and racing and as coach horses and military mounts. Today, their quiet steadiness and affectionate character make Morgans a popular choice for children and beginner riders, and excellent therapy horses.

HORSE PROFILE
Country: USA **Type:** Light
Height: 14.1–15.2 hands
Colors: Chestnut, bay, black, or brown
Personality: Athletic, calm, strong

AMERICAN STANDARDBRED

The American Standardbred may sound ordinary, but it is actually pretty special. One of the fastest horses in the world, the breed was developed in the USA in the 1870s for a sport called harness racing.

During harness racing, shown here, a horse pulls a small, two-wheeled cart around a 1-mile (1.6 km) track as quickly as it can —modern Standardbreds can zoom around a racecourse in under two minutes. As well as being speedy, Standardbreds are steady horses. Retired racers are often used in historical battle reenactments in America due to their calm and dependable natures.

HORSE PROFILE
Country: USA
Type: Light **Height:** 15–16 hands
Colors: Bay, brown, or chestnut
Personality: Steady, fast, friendly

The name Standardbred" dates back to the breed's early development. Horses were only allowed to be registered as Standardbreds if they met a certain "standard" of speed —they had to be able to trot 1 mile (1.6 km) in 2 minutes 30 seconds or less.

AMERICAN SHETLAND

Scottish Shetland ponies (p.39) arrived in America in the 1880s, and US breeders set about developing their own version of the much-loved miniature breed. They crossed Shetlands with Hackneys (p.41), Welsh ponies (p.42), and Arabs (p.88) to create a pony that was taller and more elegant than its stocky cousins.

The most popular pony breed in the USA, American Shetlands are often used to pull small buggies in shows. This allows them to display their striking high-stepping trot, which they inherited from their Hackney ancestors.

HORSE PROFILE
Country: USA
Type: Pony **Height:** 11.2 hands
Colors: All solid colors
Personality: Spirited, sweet, stylish

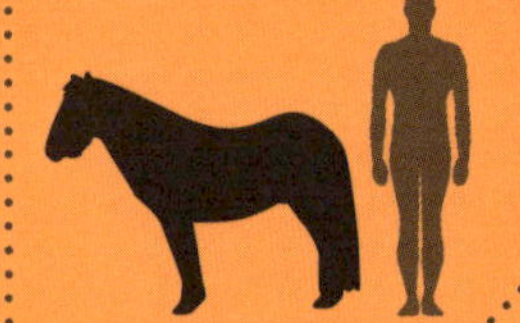

PONY OF THE AMERICAS

This beautiful breed is guaranteed to knock the spots off any other pony in the field. The Pony of the Americas was developed in Iowa in the 1950s when a Shetland stallion (p.39) was bred with an Appaloosa mare (p.22), producing a foal with a snow-white coat and black spots.

Quarter Horses (p.20), Arabs (p.88), and Welsh ponies (p.42) were later added to create a sweet-natured pony that looks like a small horse and is tailor-made for children to ride and show. Unlike Shetlands, Ponies of the Americas have narrow backs, allowing kids to reach the stirrups easily and sit comfortably in the saddle.

HORSE PROFILE
Country: USA **Type:** Pony
Height: 11.2–14 hands **Colors:** Typically black, brown, or chestnut spots
Personality: Obedient, gentle, reliable

Ponies of the Americas come in nine patterns. These include "leopard," with spots all over the body, and "blanket" with markings on the loin and hips.

ROCKY MOUNTAIN HORSE

This nimble horse can trace its history to the 1890s, when a stallion was brought from the Rocky Mountains in the western United States to the Appalachian Mountains in the east and bred with local mares. The breed was further developed in Kentucky from the 1960s onward.

What makes the Rocky Mountain horse so special and so suited to its mountain home is its "lateral gait." This means that its feet hit the ground one at a time, allowing the horse to move smoothly over bumpy ground and keep its rider comfortable. As a result, these steady horses are popular for trail riding.

HORSE PROFILE
Country: USA
Type: Light **Height:** 14–16 hands
Colors: Usually chocolate with a flaxen mane, but can be any solid color
Personality: Kind, sure-footed, trustworthy

AMERICAN SADDLEBRED

Nicknamed "the horse America made," this super-stylish breed was developed in Kentucky by crossing a now extinct horse called the Narragansett Pacer with Thoroughbreds (p.41) and, later, Morgans (p.17). The Pacer was prized for its smooth gait, which the Saddlebred has inherited.

The breed started out as a beautiful but practical farm horse, and many were used as military mounts in the American Civil War. Today, Saddlebreds are more commonly seen in the show ring, where their combination of beauty, confidence, and distinctive high-stepping trot make them the ultimate performers.

Pointed ears set close together
Big, expressive eyes
Short, strong back
Long neck
Rounded ribs
Elegant legs

HORSE PROFILE
Country: USA
Type: Light **Height:** 15–16 hands
Colors: Any color, including black, gray, chestnut, pinto, or palomino
Personality: Elegant, athletic, versatile

Saddlebreds can suffer from health problems caused by the exaggerated movements some horses are trained to perform in the show ring.

QUARTER HORSE

Saddle up and meet the Quarter Horse! A companion to cowboys and farmers, this all-American breed is one of the USA's oldest, and the nation's most popular horse. Quarter Horses were originally developed by European settlers in the 17th century to take part in quarter-mile races—short sprints that were held down the main streets of villages in the eastern US. In the early 19th century, they found a new role as settlers started to move from the eastern US to the west. These sturdy steeds were cooperative and fast on their feet, making them perfect for rounding up unruly cattle on North America's Great Plains.

Today, Quarter Horses are still prized for their "cow sense"—their built-in ability to move and guide cattle. As well as working on ranches, they're used for racing, cowboy contests known as rodeos, and trail riding.

Short, wide head

Intelligent expression

Deep chest

Compact body

Strong hindquarters

HORSE PROFILE
Country: USA
Type: Light **Height:** 15–15.3 hands
Colors: Any solid color, though the most popular is chestnut
Personality: Fast, friendly, hardworking

Quarter Horses really are fast. Some have been recorded running up to 55 miles (88.5 km) per hour!

MISSOURI FOX TROTTER

This graceful horse comes from the Ozark Mountains in Missouri and Arkansas. In the early 19th century, the local people needed horses that could work hard on their farms but also carry them comfortably over tough terrain. They bred sure-footed and strong horses together, including Morgans (p.17), Thoroughbreds (p.41), and, later, American Saddlebreds (p.19), to create this adaptable breed.

The breed is partly named after its unusual way of walking—it moves a front foot just before it moves the opposite back foot. This means its back remains very steady, making it super-smooth to ride over even the rockiest of mountains.

HORSE PROFILE
Country: USA
Type: Light **Height:** 14–16 hands
Colors: Any color, including chestnut, palomino, gray, or champagne
Personality: Strong, agile, elegant

BASHKIR CURLY

In 1898, John Damele and his son, Peter, were riding in the mountains of Nevada when they saw something unusual in a herd of Mustangs (p.56)—three of the wild horses had thick, curly coats. The Dameles tamed the curly horses and bred them with Arabs (p.88) and Morgans (p.17) to create this wonderfully woolly breed.

Their curls are the result of a special gene that has been passed down from the original Mustangs. Curlies are tough—their coats get extra-thick in winter to protect them from the cold—but they also have gentle characters to match their lamb-like looks.

Very thick, wavy or curly tail and mane
Curly eyelashes
Curly coat, which is thick in winter and thinner in summer
Low withers
Short back
Short, strong legs

HORSE PROFILE
Country: USA
Type: Light **Height:** 15 hands
Colors: Any color, though often chestnut, gray, bay, or black
Personality: Intelligent, calm, hardy

CAYUSE INDIAN PONY

This extremely rare breed takes its name from the Cayuse, an Indigenous group who originally lived in the valleys and mountains of the American Northwest. The Cayuse, such as the rider shown here in traditional dress, were known for their incredible horse skills. They used their horses to hunt bison, fight, trade, and travel.

Cayuse Indian Ponies are thought to have descended from Percherons (p.50) that were brought to America from Canada by French settlers. The Cayuse possibly crossed these powerful horses with lighter, Spanish breeds to create their small, strong ponies. Said to be capable of carrying their riders from dawn to dusk without stopping, the endurance of Cayuse Indian Ponies was the stuff of legend.

Only a small number of these special horses are thought to survive in California and Kentucky, where fans are trying to build a herd and protect them from extinction.

Sloped pasterns give the pony a broken walking gait, which makes it comfortable to ride.

HORSE PROFILE
Country: USA
Type: Pony **Height:** 14 hands
Colors: Any color **Personality:** Brave, fast, strong

APPALOOSA

If you want a horse that stands out from the crowd, you've turned to the right page. The stunning Appaloosa is thought to have descended from Spanish horses brought to North America in the 17th century and adopted by the Indigenous Nez Perce people. The Nez Perce were skilled horse breeders, who picked only the strongest, fastest, and hardiest horses.

Appaloosa horses almost became extinct in the 1870s, when the US government stole Nez Perce land. Admirers saved the breed in the 1930s and today these beautiful and one-of-a-kind horses are used for riding, racing, and jumping all over the world.

HORSE PROFILE
Country: USA
Type: Light **Height:** 14.2–15.2 hands
Colors: Various spotty patterns
Personality: Biddable, hardy, loyal

It's thought the name Appaloosa comes from the Palouse River, which runs through the land of the Nez Perce people. Over time "Palouse" became "Appaloosa."

GALICEÑO

Tiny but tough sums up this rare Mexican breed. The Galiceño (you say it "gal-eh-seen-yo") is descended from Spanish and Portuguese horses brought to the Americas by European settlers in the 16th century. These little horses had to be extra-hardy to survive the voyage across the Atlantic Ocean, and when they reached Mexico, many were used for work in mines and on farms. Others were left to roam free and were adopted by local people.

Over the centuries, the horses developed naturally in Mexico before catching the attention of breeders in America in the 1950s. Many were then imported to the USA, and the Galiceño became an official breed in 1958.

Despite being the size of a pony, Galiceños have horse-like proportions and kindly natures, making them a great choice for young riders. These sturdy steeds are perfectly capable of carrying adults, too. Their strength and inquisitiveness mean Galiceños are happy to try their hoof at all sorts of activities, from dressage and jumping to pulling carts and cattle driving.

The breed's name comes from an area of Spain called Galicia, reflecting its European roots.

HORSE PROFILE

Country: Mexico
Type: Pony **Height:** 12–13.2 hands
Colors: Any solid colors, often black, bay, or chestnut
Personality: Friendly, hardy, curious

FABULOUS FOALS

There's nothing cuter than a tiny foal taking its first frolic in a field. But baby horses don't stay little for long. A lot goes on in the first year of a horse's life, and there are important milestones each foal should experience so it can grow into a healthy and happy adult. Let's follow one foal for a year and see what she gets up to.

Just born

Meet Willow. This little foal has just been born. Her mother licks Willow to warm her up and establish their bond. Within an hour, Willow has stood up, taken her first wobbly steps, and had her first drink of milk from her mom. This first milk is filled with nutrients that will help Willow grow, as well as antibodies that will protect her from infection.

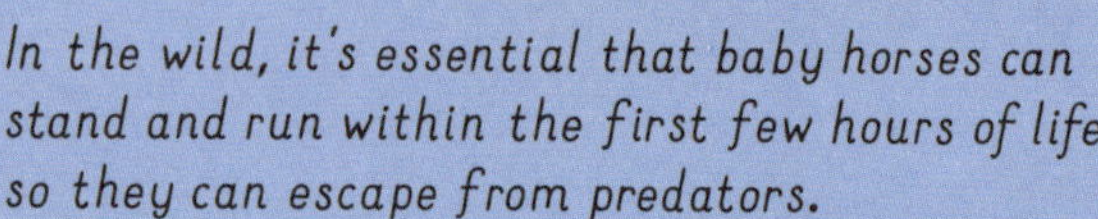

In the wild, it's essential that baby horses can stand and run within the first few hours of life so they can escape from predators.

Heading outdoors: I week old

Willow spends at least a third of her day snoozing and will suckle milk from her mom two or three times an hour. Willow and her mom are let out of their stable each day to enjoy some gentle exercise. The little foal stays close to her mom, but might try a short canter if she's feeling confident! Willow's human owners gently stroke her, so she gets used to being handled by people.

Trying new things: 2-4 weeks

By now, Willow has had her first taste of solid food, taking a nibble of her mom's hay—mmm, grassy! She will also play with her mom to develop social skills. When she is about four weeks old, she will be seen by a horse foot expert (known as a farrier), who will check that her hooves are developing properly and give Willow her first gentle trim.

Young foals sometimes eat their mom's poop! Although this sounds gross, it's thought this helps the foal to develop healthy gut bacteria.

Independent Willow: 4-7 months

Willow is becoming more independent and developing grown-up-horse behaviors. She'll spend less time playing and more time grazing, for example. Willow is still drinking her mom's milk, but she is getting most of her nutrients from grass and feed. At six months, Willow will be given her first vaccinations by a vet to protect her from horse diseases.

Weaning: 8-12 months

Willow now gets her nutrients from solid food and will gradually stop drinking mom's milk—a process known as weaning. Willow's owners encourage her to spend more time with other horses and less time with her mom. They also introduce some basic training, such as walking on a lead, being groomed, and wearing a horse blanket.

Making friends: 2-3 months

Willow is becoming much more confident and spends more time playing with other foals in the field—it's so much fun, she can't help jumping and bucking with excitement! Playtime helps Willow to develop social bonds and learn boundaries. Willow and her friends may also groom one another to strengthen their relationships.

Happy birthday, Willow!: 1 year old

Willow is now a "yearling." Her owners continue gentle training so she will become comfortable around humans. She'll also spend lots of time with other yearlings in the field to help her develop into a happy, confident young horse. She'll continue to grow through her "teenage years" and become an adult when she is around four or five years old.

SOUTH AMERICA

All horses in South America are descended from stallions and mares that were brought to the continent by Europeans in the 16th century. In the centuries since, these horses have undergone incredible transformations that have resulted in stylish, spirited breeds. In this chapter, we'll meet ponies left to roam wild in the deep forests of Brazil, equines that carry Argentine cowboys (gauchos) across endless plains, and Peruvian horses with one-of-a-kind footwork. Get ready for an epic ride!

Modern horses were introduced to South America by Spanish invaders called conquistadors, from the 1530s, like the one shown here. These soldiers used their horses to travel across the continent and take control of Indigenous lands and empires by force. The conquistadors' horses included Barbs (p.76) and Andalusians (p.60).

CAMPEIRO
BRAZIL

The Argentine Criollo is renowned for its stamina. Each year, breeders take part in an endurance race called La Marcha, which covers 466 miles (750 km) over two weeks, to show off their horses' long-distance skills.

PAMPA HORSE
BRAZIL

ARGENTINE CRIOLLO
ARGENTINA

CHILEAN HORSE
CHILE

ARGENTINE POLO PONY
ARGENTINA

FALABELLA
ARGENTINA

Although they have much smaller bodies than regular horses, Falabellas have hearts that are as big as a larger horse. It's thought this helps give them a particularly long lifespan—Falabellas typically live for between 40 and 45 years.

A LAND OF HORSES

Horses were prized by the conquistadors, but many were lost or abandoned as the soldiers made their way across the continent. These horses eventually found a new home with South America's Indigenous peoples.

The Tehuelche, for example, were a group of people in Patagonia—a region of enormous mountains and grasslands at the southern tip of South America. By the 18th century, horses had become an essential part of their lives and culture. Horses helped the Tehuelche to navigate the difficult landscape more easily, allowing them to hunt, travel, and trade with other Indigenous groups in the north.

A Tehuelche rider

PERUVIAN PASO

You can recognize this horse by the way it moves. The Peruvian Paso has an incredibly smooth and special way of walking—it has a slow, even gait, known as *paso llano*. During *paso llano* the horse may also swing its front legs outward, creating a gentle rolling movement (called *termino*).

These signature moves had a practical purpose. The Peruvian Paso is descended from Spanish horses brought to South America by conquistadors in the 16th century. They were used to carry riders over Peru's harsh deserts and mountains, and to work on vast ranches. As well as being hardy and easy to handle, they had to have a smooth gait so a rider could sit in the saddle for a long time without bouncing around.

Because they are so comfortable to ride, Peruvian Pasos make excellent trail horses. They are also sought after by riders with hip or back pain. In fact, this horse is so steady, it's said that you can hold a glass of water while riding a Peruvian Paso and never spill a drop!

Short, muscular neck
Broad back
Confident, proud expression
Termino movement
Flexible joints
Glossy mane and tail
Long, powerful hind legs

HORSE PROFILE
Country: Peru
Type: Light **Height:** 14.1–15.2 hands
Colors: Any color, including chestnut, bay, black, palomino, or gray
Personality: Friendly, confident, stylish

Breeders of Peruvian Pasos look for horses with brio. Horses that have brio have a natural confidence and controlled energy, without being fiery or hard to handle.

PASO FINO

The beautiful Paso Fino is descended from Spanish horses, including Andalusians (p.60) and an extinct breed called the Jennet, which were brought to the Caribbean and Central and South America by Europeans. Two versions of the breed were developed in Colombia and Puerto Rico, and today, the Colombian Paso Fino is the more widespread.

Like the Peruvian Paso (see opposite), the Paso Fino has a natural lateral gait, which makes the horse extremely comfortable to ride—*paso fino* means "fine step" in Spanish. Originally used to carry landowners around their vast plantations, these sure-footed horses are now used for a variety of activities, including trail riding, endurance competitions, and parades.

The Paso Fino has a four-beat lateral gait that is performed at three different speeds—classic fino (slow), paso corto (moderate speed), and paso largo (fast).

HORSE PROFILE
Country: Colombia and Puerto Rico
Type: Light **Height:** 13–15.2 hands
Colors: Any color
Personality: Sensible, people-orientated, athletic

CHILEAN HORSE

The national horse of Chile, these horses have been the companions of the country's *huasos* (skilled horseback riders) for centuries and are South America's oldest registered breed. They are descended from Spanish horses that were imported to Chile from Peru in the 16th century, and then developed in the country in isolation.

As a result, they are perfectly adapted to the extreme landscapes of their home nation. Bred to control cattle in Chile's towering mountains and windswept plains, Chilean Horses are tough, agile, and not easily spooked. They are still used to work cattle and for rodeos and are a great choice for mountain trail riding.

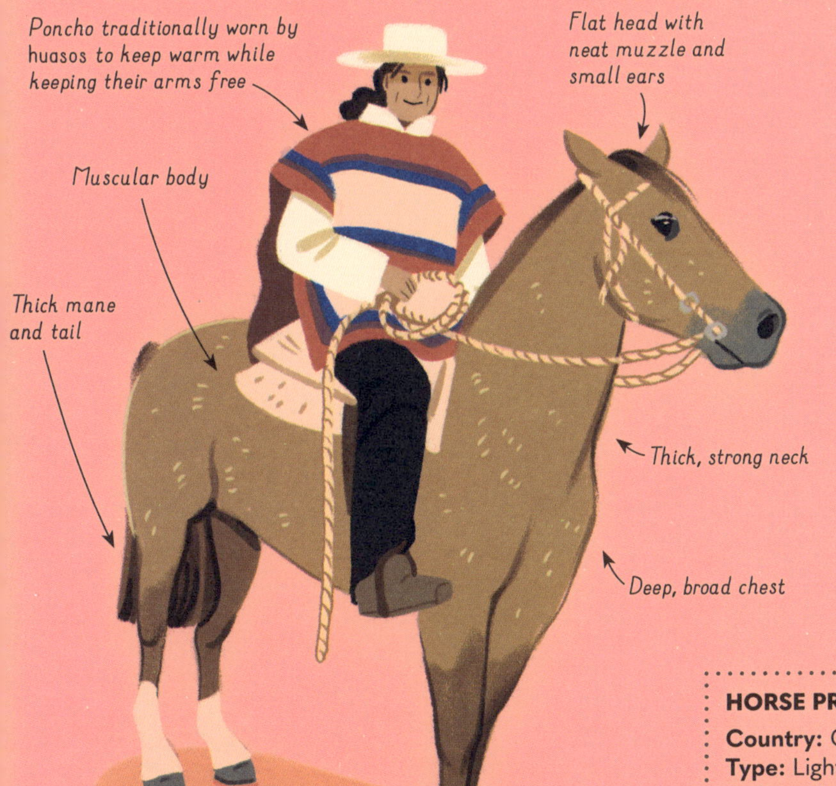

HORSE PROFILE
Country: Chile
Type: Light **Height:** Around 14.3 hands
Colors: Any color, though black or chestnut are common
Personality: Intelligent, strong, good-natured

Two Argentine Criollos named Gato and Mancha took part in an epic ride from Buenos Aires in Argentina to New York in the USA between 1925 and 1928—a distance of over 10,000 miles (16,000 km).

ARGENTINE CRIOLLO

Not many horses have the skill to trek across the mountains of Patagonia, or the stamina to race for hours through the grasslands of the Pampas . . . except the Argentine Criollo. These horses are brave, tough, and free-spirited, just like the legendary *gauchos* (Argentine cowboys) who ride them, such as the rider in this image, shown wearing traditional dress.

Criollos are descended from a group of Spanish horses that were brought to Argentina in the 1530s by European explorers and left to fend for themselves. The offspring of these horses were later recaptured and tamed by Spanish settlers and local people. In the time they'd been wild, the horses had become perfectly adapted to Argentina's extreme climate. A Criollo can work through hot summers and bitterly cold winters, survive on little food and water, is resistant to many common horse diseases, and lives for at least 30 years.

HORSE PROFILE
Country: Argentina
Type: Light **Height:** 14–15 hands
Colors: Any color, except paint
Personality: Strong, independent, hardworking

Criollos were used to carry riders over tricky terrain to round up cattle and tend to land. They are still used as cattle horses, as well as for trail riding and rodeos. Because of their incredible endurance, they have been used for long-distance journeys and races.

ARGENTINE POLO PONY

These lightning-quick horses are bred to play a sport called polo, where teams on horseback use a long mallet to hit a ball through a goal (a bit like playing hockey on a horse).

When the sport arrived in South America in the late 19th century, Argentinian breeders decided to create their own polo pony. They combined the stamina and toughness of the Criollo (see opposite) with the swiftness of the Thoroughbred (p.41) to create a breed that can twist and turn in a split second and has an instinctive talent for the game. Despite having "Pony" in their name, this is a light horse breed.

HORSE PROFILE
Country: Argentina **Type:** Light
Height: 14.2–15 hands
Colors: Any color but often bay
Personality: Fast, agile, bold

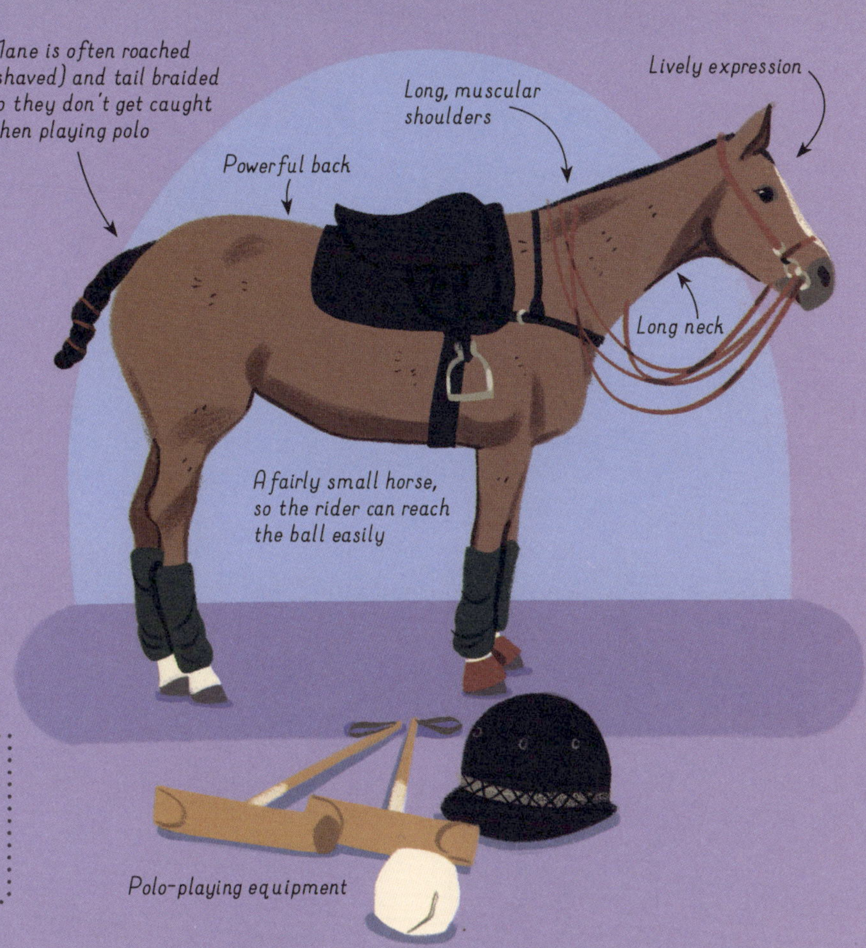

FALABELLA

Meet one of the smallest horses in the world. Falabellas are descended from Spanish horses brought to Argentina in the 16th century, then left to roam free on the Pampas (grassy plains). Centuries of wandering long distances to find food, and coping with high winds and hot summers, created horses that were small, strong, and spirited. Many were adopted by the Indigenous Mapuche people, who sold a herd to horse breeders in the 19th century—the modern Falabella is descended from this herd. Shetland Ponies (p.39), small Thoroughbreds (p.41), and Criollos (p.30) were used to perfect the breed.

Today's Falabellas make sweet pets who love to be around people. Thanks to their portable size, they can access places that regular-sized horses can't—such as schools and care homes—and are often used as therapy and even guide horses.

HORSE PROFILE
Country: Argentina
Type: Pony **Height:** 8 hands
Colors: All colors, including spotted
Personality: Clever, friendly, gentle

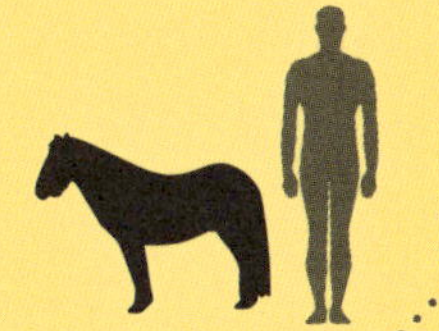

MANGALARGA MARCHADOR

The national horse of Brazil, this breed has its origins in the late 18th century, when a Portuguese stallion called Sublime was brought to the country and bred with Spanish Jennets and Andalusians (p.60). The Jennet was renowned for its smooth gait, which it passed on to the Marchador.

Although these horses look proud, they don't mind getting their hooves muddy. They are often seen helping farmers herd cattle on Brazilian ranches, as well as being used in sports such as polo, cross-country racing, and show jumping.

HORSE PROFILE
Country: Brazil
Type: Light **Height:** 14.2–16 hands
Colors: All colors, including gray, chestnut, black, palomino, or paint
Personality: Sensible, agile, gentle

CAMPOLINA

With its majestic body and exaggerated nose, the Campolina has a horsey style all of its own. These unusual-looking horses are named after a farmer, Cassiano Campolina, who developed them in the 1870s. He crossed a Barb mare (p.76) with an Andalusian stallion (p.60), and their colt became the founding horse of the breed. Clydesdales (p.38) were later introduced for strength, and Holsteiners (p.54) and Marchadors (see above) for flair and elegance.

Campolinas are typically used for leisure riding and make particularly comfortable rides on long-distance trails thanks to their smooth gait. They are also a popular choice for dressage in Brazil.

Long, expressive ears
Arched neck
Muscular body
Curved face
Strong legs

HORSE PROFILE
Country: Brazil
Type: Light **Height:** 15–15.2 hands
Colors: Any color, but silver-gray is very popular
Personality: Good-tempered, confident, graceful

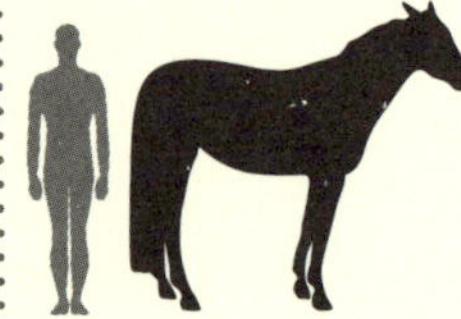

Brazil is home to around 85,000 of these striking horses.

CAMPEIRO

In the south of Brazil, a dense forest of pine trees once stretched for hundreds of square miles over mountains and plateaus. Here in the 16th century, a group of Spanish explorers lost some of their horses. Left to roam among the spiky trees for hundreds of years, the descendants of these mares and stallions became small, tough, and used to thinking for themselves.

From the 1700s onward, many of these horses were tamed, selectively bred for their natural ambling gait, and developed into the breed known today as the Campeiro. Often used for leisure riding and for pulling light loads, Campeiros also make good cattle horses due to their independence and intelligence.

HORSE PROFILE
Country: Brazil
Type: Light **Height:** 14.1–15.1 hands
Colors: Any color, but most common are chestnut, bay, or gray
Personality: Clever, friendly, agile

PAMPA HORSE

The Pampa Horse is Brazil's spotted (or pinto) breed. Its origins are unclear—it's thought the breed developed from horses brought to Brazil by European settlers in the 16th century and were refined with other South American horses, such as the Marchador (see opposite) and the Criollo (p.30).

The Pampa Horse's most obvious feature is its spectacular coat, which is a dazzling white with black- or brown-colored patches. It has a natural gait, making it very easy to ride. As well as being used for leisure riding, these multitalented horses can be seen working on Brazilian farms and taking part in long-distance treks.

HORSE PROFILE
Country: Brazil
Type: Light **Height:** 14–14.2 hands
Colors: Pinto pattern of white and dark colors
Personality: Energetic, good-natured, adaptable

DONKEYS, MULES, AND HINNIES

Compared to a dazzling palomino or a dashing Thoroughbred, a little gray donkey looks pretty ordinary. But donkeys and their relatives—mules and hinnies—are extraordinary equines. With around 60 million donkeys and mules in the world today, and over 180 donkey breeds, these intelligent, gentle, and hardworking animals deserve to be celebrated.

DONKEY WORLD

Donkeys have lived and worked alongside us for at least 6,000 years. They are descended from African wild asses (p.80) that were first tamed in northeast Africa, before being brought to Europe and Asia. These humble animals transformed human lives during ancient times, helping farmers to plow fields and carrying people and goods over long distances.

Because their wild ancestors lived in deserts and savannas, donkeys can survive in difficult conditions. As well as being tough, they are amazingly strong. Millions of donkeys are still used to carry loads and work the land, especially in Africa and Asia.

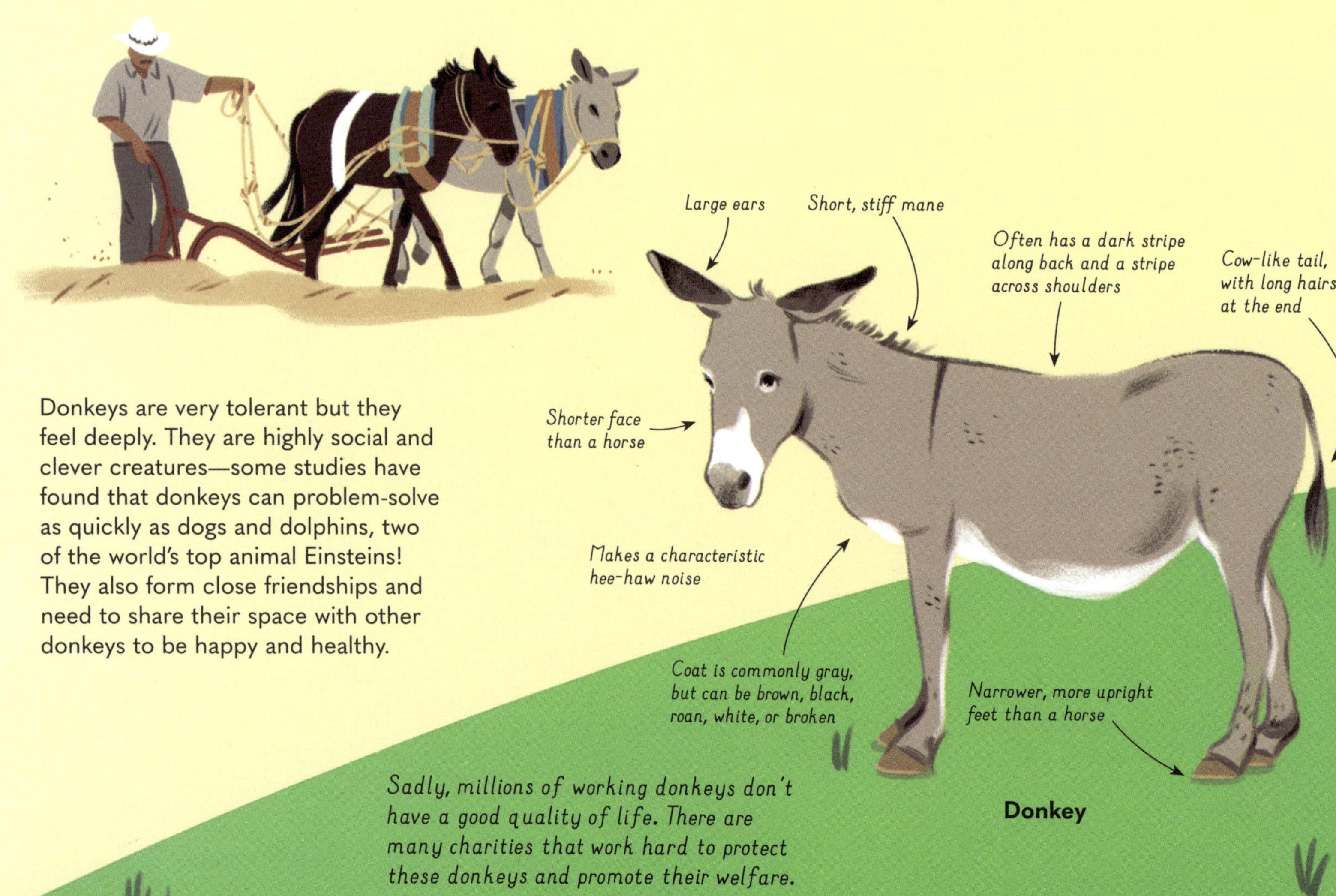

Donkey

Donkeys are very tolerant but they feel deeply. They are highly social and clever creatures—some studies have found that donkeys can problem-solve as quickly as dogs and dolphins, two of the world's top animal Einsteins! They also form close friendships and need to share their space with other donkeys to be happy and healthy.

Sadly, millions of working donkeys don't have a good quality of life. There are many charities that work hard to protect these donkeys and promote their welfare.

MULES RULE!

Because horses and donkeys are closely related, they can breed with one another and have young that are known as hybrids. A mule is the hybrid offspring of a male donkey and a female horse. A hinny is the result of a male horse breeding with a female donkey.

How can you tell if you're petting a mule or a hinny? A mule has the head of a donkey and the body of a horse, while a hinny has a horse-like head and a donkey body. Hinnies tend to be more horsey in their behavior, too, whereas mules take after their donkey parent.

Like donkeys, mules and hinnies have been used for thousands of years to carry loads and help with farmwork. Mules can pull even heavier loads than donkeys. These tough animals are known for being strong-minded, but their stubbornness is actually a reflection of their intelligence—mules like to think before they do something, making them much safer to ride over tough terrain than horses.

Long ears and donkey-like head

Thin tail and mane

Strong, horse-like body

Long, thin legs

Tough hooves

Mule

Short ears

Horse-like head

Usually has a donkey-like body

Longer mane and tail compared to a mule

Hinny

Both mules and hinnies make a noise that's half donkey hee-haw, half horsey whinny.

Mules and hinnies have a trait called hybrid vigor. This is when a crossbreed animal is stronger and healthier than its parents. Mules and hinnies are often very resistant to common horse and donkey illnesses, for example.

1. **CLYDESDALE** – SCOTLAND, UK
2. **SHETLAND** – SCOTLAND, UK
3. **HIGHLAND** – SCOTLAND, UK
4. **SHIRE** – ENGLAND, UK
5. **THOROUGHBRED** – ENGLAND, UK
6. **HACKNEY** – ENGLAND, UK
7. **WELSH PONIES AND COBS** – WALES, UK
8. **IRISH DRAFT** – IRELAND
9. **CONNEMARA** – IRELAND
10. **ICELANDIC** – ICELAND
11. **FJORD** – NORWAY
12. **JUTLAND** – DENMARK
13. **SWEDISH WARMBLOOD** – SWEDEN
14. **FINNISH HORSE** – FINLAND
15. **FRIESIAN** – THE NETHERLANDS
16. **BELGIAN WARMBLOOD** – BELGIUM
17. **PERCHERON** – FRANCE
18. **NORMAN COB** – FRANCE
19. **SELLE FRANCAIS** – FRANCE
20. **FRENCH TROTTER** – FRANCE
21. **ARDENNAIS** – FRANCE
22. **BRETON** – FRANCE
23. **BOULONNAIS** – FRANCE
24. **OLDENBURGER** – GERMANY
25. **HOLSTEINER** – GERMANY
26. **HANOVERIAN** – GERMANY
27. **HAFLINGER** – AUSTRIA

The Finnish Horse is not a heavy breed, but it is exceptionally strong. This compact horse can pull up to twice its own weight!

In Irish folklore, horses are associated with luck and good fortune. Farmers would get their horses to walk over fields of newly sown seeds, to ensure a successful harvest.

In the 1920s, several Jutland horses were bought by the Carlsberg brewery in Copenhagen to haul barrels and deliver cartloads of beer. A team of Jutlands can still be spotted calmly pulling a Carlsberg cart through the city's streets.

Shires are still sometimes used by farmers as an environmentally friendly alternative to tractors. In London, UK, teams of Shires are used to plow and reseed meadows in the city's parks.

Some historians believe England's first Norman king, William the Conqueror, rode a Friesian at the Battle of Hastings in 1066.

EUROPE (North & West)

Northern and Western Europe are the birthplace of some of the world's oldest and best-loved breeds. This is the home of horsey heavyweights, such as the Shire and Percheron, nimble-hoofed athletes, such as the Thoroughbred and Holsteiner, and plucky ponies, like the Shetland and Welsh Mountain. As well as being bred for special roles, many of these horses were developed to thrive in certain environments—from Norwegian fjords and Austrian mountains to rolling English hills and Finnish pine forests.

CLYDESDALE

Scotland's heavy horse gets its name from the rolling countryside that surrounds the River Clyde. The handsome and hardworking Clydesdale has its origins in the early 18th century, when stallions from Belgium and the Netherlands were brought to the area and bred with local mares. Another giant breed, the Shire (p.40), was later added to the mix.

A Clydesdale's original job was to pull heavy farm equipment, but the breed's strength, stamina, and obedient nature saw these horses being put to use in all manner of ways—from hauling coal and milk wagons to pulling trams in towns. Their saucepan-sized hooves meant Clydesdales were particularly suited to long days trudging through hard city streets, and they were a familiar sight in urban areas into the 20th century.

Wide forehead with white blaze

Sloped shoulders

Long legs with a characteristic high-stepping trot

Strong, muscular body

Flowing, silky hairs (called feathers) on lower legs

Enormous hooves

HORSE PROFILE
Country: Scotland, UK
Type: Heavy **Height:** 16.2–18 hands
Colors: Bay, brown, or black, with white markings
Personality: Gentle, sensible, strong

By the 1950s, Clydesdales had been largely replaced on farms and roads by tractors and trucks, and the breed was at risk of extinction. They are still a rare breed today, but if you're lucky, you can see these magnificent horses strutting their stuff in parades or country shows.

SHETLAND PONY

The rugged Shetland Islands off the north coast of Scotland have been home to small ponies since the Bronze Age (around 4,000 years ago). The modern Shetland was developed in isolation there. They were bred to be incredibly tough, both to survive the islands' harsh climate and to perform difficult jobs. They were originally used to lug carts of seaweed and peat (a soil-like material used as fuel). During the 19th century, they were also taken to the mainland to work in coal mines.

Beneath their shaggy manes, Shetlands' black eyes glitter with determination—this is a clever breed with a spirit to match its strength. Although they have a stubborn side, Shetlands are gentle animals and their small size and sturdiness makes them popular riding ponies for young children.

HORSE PROFILE

Country: Scotland, UK
Type: Pony **Height:** 10.2 hands
Colors: Any color/pattern, except spotted
Personality: Intelligent, active, strong-willed

HIGHLAND

The earliest record of ponies in the Scottish Highlands dates back to 800 BCE, when a group of people called the Picts carved images of their horses onto stones. The Highland looks similar to these ancient horses. However, French and Spanish horses, Arabs (p.88), and Clydesdales (see opposite) have been used over the last 500 years to refine the breed.

Perfectly adapted to the moors and mountains of Scotland's highlands and islands, these powerful, all-weather ponies were built for a life hauling timber through forests or carrying hunting equipment up hills. Prized for their calm nature, Highlands make an excellent choice for first-time or nervous riders.

HORSE PROFILE

Country: Scotland, UK
Type: Pony **Height:** 13–14.2 hands
Colors: Various shades of dun, as well as gray, brown, black, bay, or chestnut
Personality: Hardy, calm, adaptable

SHIRE

Standing up to 19 hands high, the Shire is the world's tallest horse. This gentle giant is named after the counties ("shires") in England, where it was developed in the 18th century, but its history goes back much further. The Shire is descended from the English Great Horse, an enormous breed that was ridden by medieval knights. To carry a knight in armor, with a combined weight of 400 lbs. (180 kg), these horses had to be incredibly strong, as well as brave, to cope with the chaos of battle.

In the 16th century, Great Horses found a new role pulling plows on farms. Over the next 200 years, they were mixed with Belgian and Dutch breeds to create the Shire. By the 19th century, they had become part of everyday life in Britain. Millions were used to pull wagons in cities, carry cargo from docks, and tow barges along canals, as shown below. However, their numbers declined from the 1950s, when advances in technology meant the horses were no longer needed for many of their jobs.

HORSE PROFILE
Country: England
Type: Heavy **Height:** 17–19 hands
Colors: Black, brown, bay, or gray
Personality: Loyal, hardworking, kindly

With fewer than 3,000 alive today, these magnificent horses are a rare but unmistakable sight.

THOROUGHBRED

The king of the racetrack, the Thoroughbred was born to run. These speed machines have their origins in the 17th and 18th centuries, when horse racing became a popular hobby among English aristocrats. Wealthy stable owners bred fast English horses with Arabs (p.88), Barbs (p.76), and Turkish breeds to develop unbeatable horsey athletes.

Thoroughbreds can hit a top speed of 40–44 miles (64–70 km) per hour thanks to their streamlined bodies, long strides, and powerful back legs, which propel them around a racecourse. Retired Thoroughbreds can be used for general riding but they need a very experienced owner—because their whole life is geared toward racing, they can be restless and easily spooked.

HORSE PROFILE

Country: England **Type:** Light
Height: 15–17 hands
Colors: Usually bay, chestnut, brown, black, or gray
Personality: Athletic, spirited, bold

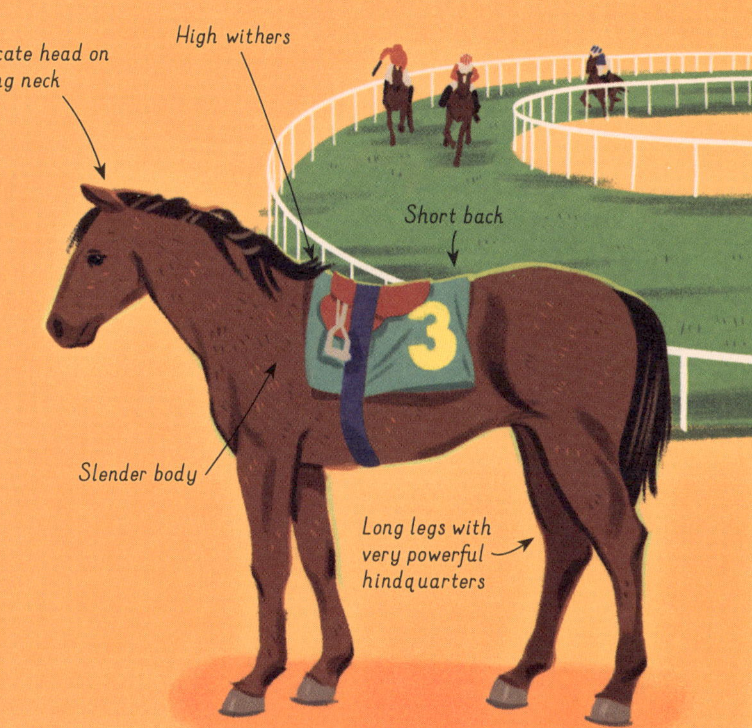

Horse racing pushes horses to their physical limits. It comes with the risk of injury and can lead to health problems for Thoroughbreds.

HACKNEY

The Hackney is a stunning horse that combines strength with style. It originated in the 18th and 19th centuries when roads improved and there was an increased demand for horses to pull carriages, as shown on the left. Hackneys were perfect for the job because they could cover a lot of ground quickly—in 1800, a Hackney mare called Phenomena was recorded trotting 17 miles (27 km) in 53 minutes.

Hackneys were also a status symbol, with their snappy, high-stepping trot setting them apart from the average horse on the road. Hackneys are rare nowadays, but you can still see them demonstrating their nimble step and carriage skills in the show ring.

HORSE PROFILE

Country: England
Type: Light **Height:** 14.2–16.2 hands
Colors: Any solid color, including brown, chestnut, bay, or black
Personality: Elegant, active, alert

WELSH PONIES AND COBS

The wild hills of Wales are the birthplace of four much-loved breeds. Because they are so closely related, Welsh breeds are grouped into "sections" based on height: the Welsh Mountain Pony (Section A), Welsh Pony (Section B), Welsh Pony of Cob Type (Section C), and Welsh Cob (Section D).

The Welsh Mountain Pony is the smallest and the breed from which the three others developed. This pretty pony can trace its history to small Celtic horses, which were brought to Wales during the Bronze Age (around 4,000 years ago). The modern breed was refined in the 18th century, when tough Welsh mares were crossed with dainty Thoroughbred (p.41) and Arab (p.88) stallions. Sure-footed, friendly, and not easily spooked, they make outstanding ponies for children.

HORSE PROFILE

Country: Wales **Types:** Pony and Light
Height: 12 hands (Section A), 12–13.2 hands (Sections B and C), over 13.2 hands (Section D)
Colors: Any color except piebald or skewbald
Personality: Hardy, spirited, people-loving

The Welsh Cob is the largest Welsh breed and was developed to work on hilltop farms. Its compact size, courage, and strength meant it was often used in coal mines in the 19th century and to carry soldiers and pull heavy guns during wars. Today, they excel in many sports, including dressage and driving.

IRISH DRAFT

The Irish Draft is the national horse of Ireland. It has its origins in war horses that were brought from France and Belgium in the 12th century and crossed with a now-extinct breed called the Irish Hobby.

The breed is lighter than the "draft" part of its name suggests (as in pulling a heavy load). They were developed over centuries to be all-purpose farmworkers—strong enough to pull a plow, agile enough to be ridden across the countryside, and stylish enough to take a cart into town.

HORSE PROFILE
Country: Ireland **Type:** Light
Height: 15.2–16.3 hands
Colors: Any solid color, including gray, bay, brown, black, or dun
Personality: Adaptable, strong, sensible

Irish Drafts are excellent jumpers and are often bred with Thoroughbreds (p.41) to create Irish Sport Horses, which are especially good at show jumping and dressage.

CONNEMARA

Connemara in the west of Ireland is a land of lonely mountains and craggy moors. The exact origins of the breed are unclear. One theory is that the ancestors of today's Connemara ponies may have been brought to Ireland by the Vikings. Over centuries, the ponies became perfectly adapted to their windswept home. When Spanish warships were wrecked on the coast in the 1580s, several Andalusian horses (p.60) escaped and bred with the local ponies, adding beauty to this rugged breed.

HORSE PROFILE
Country: Ireland
Type: Pony **Height:** 12.2–14.2 hands
Colors: Gray, black, bay, brown, dun, or occasionally roan, palomino, or cream
Personality: Hardy, intelligent, dependable

These robust ponies have steady, sweet characters that make them suitable for riders of all ages. They are also used for show jumping, dressage, and endurance riding.

ICELANDIC

The first thing you need to know about the Icelandic is never call it a pony! Despite standing around 13 hands high, Icelanders always refer to this spirited and hardy breed as a horse.

The ancestors of these little horses first set hoof on the volcanic island of Iceland in the 9th century, when they were brought from Norway and Britain by Viking settlers. A law was soon passed forbidding the introduction of any other horse breeds to the country, meaning the Icelandic has stayed remarkably pure and unchanged to this day. Many Icelandics are left to roam freely and live semi-wild on the island.

Iceland's harsh climate and rocky landscape would be a challenge for the sturdiest of horses, but the Icelandic is perfectly adapted to thrive here. They are strong swimmers and sure-footed and grow a thick double coat in winter to protect them from the cold.

Traditionally, the horses were used by Icelandic people to herd sheep. Today, they take part in show jumping, cross-country racing, and dressage. They are also used for tourist rides in Iceland —although small, they are happy carrying adult riders across the bumpiest of terrain.

HORSE PROFILE

Country: Iceland
Type: Pony **Height:** 12–14 hands
Colors: Any coat color, including chestnut, dun, palomino, roan, or black
Personality: Tough, free-spirited, intelligent

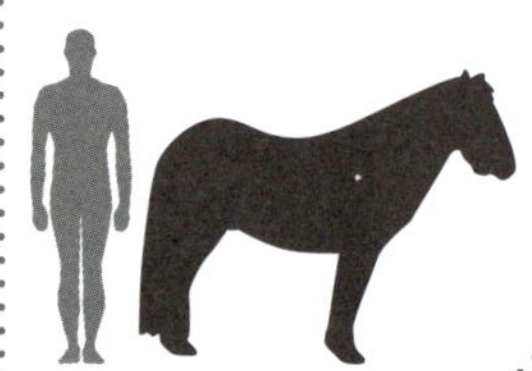

FJORD

The Fjord ("fee-ord") comes from Norway's west coast, where deep channels called fjords slice through mountains. These tough horses (despite being pony-sized, they are considered horses) have been shaped by this environment for 4,000 years. It's thought their ancestors were used by the Vikings as warhorses before they became an essential part of Norwegian life, pulling plows on mountain farms and hauling logs through forests.

Kind expression

Small, alert ears

The horse's mane is usually cut short (or "hogged") to show off the black stripe of hair that runs from the top of its head to the tip of its tail.

Round, barrel-like body

Arched neck

Wild horse markings, including a dorsal stripe and striped legs

Light feathering around hard hooves

HORSE PROFILE

Country: Norway
Type: Light **Height:** 13–14 hands
Colors: Dun
Personality: Courageous, robust, good-natured

If you have a chance to ride a Fjord, take it; you couldn't ask for a trustier friend to guide you through the mountains.

JUTLAND

This powerful breed comes from the Jutland Peninsula in Denmark. It's thought they were developed here from at least the 12th century, when knights relied on these heavy horses to carry them (and their armor) into battle.

By the mid-19th century, Jutlands had been refined to make them more suited to farmwork. Breeders crossed local mares with a British stallion that was part Shire (p.40) and part Suffolk Punch (p.46). Today's Jutlands share the Suffolk's stout build, chestnut coat, and soft nature.

Muscular and extremely powerful hindquarters

Short, arched neck

Round body

Wide, strong chest

Heavy feathering around feet

Short legs

HORSE PROFILE

Country: Denmark
Type: Heavy **Height:** 15–16.1 hands
Colors: Usually chestnut with flaxen mane and tail
Personality: Strong, hardworking, kind

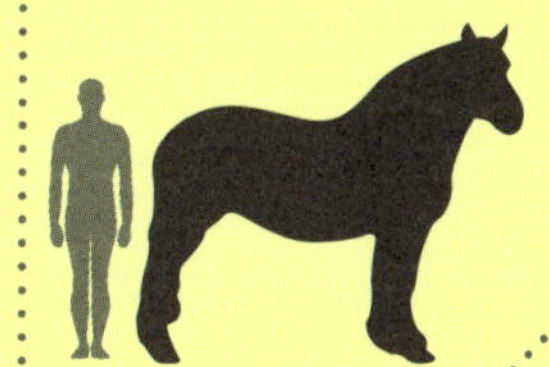

WORKING HORSES

Imagine you lived 150 years ago. All around you would be busy horses hard at work—pulling coaches, barges, and trains, plowing the land, and even delivering letters. Today, horses have been replaced by machines in most of their original roles, but many still perform important jobs around the world. Let's take a look at a few.

Many countries still rely on horses for farmwork and transportation. There are over 100 million working horses, ponies, donkeys, and mules in the world today. They are not always well cared-for. Charities such as Brooke and World Horse Welfare work hard to help them.

ECO-FRIENDLY FARMING

In some parts of the world, horses are used as eco-friendly alternatives to tractors. The Suffolk Punch was developed on farms in England in the 18th century to pull enormous loads, but the breed declined when machines were introduced in the 20th century. Today, Suffolks are used to manage woods and farmland in parts of the UK. They help to keep the land healthy as they don't damage the soil as much as a vehicle's tires. Plus, they provide a natural fertilizer through their poop!

POLICE HORSES

These sensible horses carry police officers on patrol, helping them see over crowds and quickly reach people who are hurt or causing trouble. Police officers around the world still use horses to keep the peace on streets or at busy events. Heavy horses, such as Percherons (p.50), are valued for their powerful presence and calmness, while lighter breeds, such as Thoroughbreds (p.41), are chosen for their speed.

Most horses were bred to do jobs. Heavy (or "draft") horses did tough lifting and pulling tasks, lighter breeds were used to carry people or goods, and ponies worked in places where bigger horses couldn't go, such as mines.

THERAPY HORSES

These very special equines are trained to provide physical and emotional support to people. All sorts of breeds can be therapy horses, but they need to be gentle and steady. Horses with smooth gaits, such as Missouri Fox Trotters (p.21), are used for riding therapies, helping people develop coordination and confidence. Due to their kind nature, heavy breeds, such as Clydesdales (p.38), are often used for non-riding sessions, when people spend time stroking or walking a horse.

Horses have understudies and stunt doubles, just like human actors do. In the 2011 film War Horse, the main horse character, Joey, was played by 14 different horses.

FILM AND TV HORSES

Horses regularly appear on movie theater and TV screens in everything from Westerns to period dramas. Months of careful training go into preparing horses for film roles. Some, like human movie extras, perform a role in the background and have to be calm and obedient so actors can film their scenes without any hiccups. Others are specially trained to perform their own stunts, including rearing up, falling down, and jumping over obstacles.

ROYAL HORSES

Horses add stateliness to royal ceremonies around the world. One of the most famous horsey spectacles is Trooping the Color, which takes place in London, UK, every year to celebrate the British monarch's birthday. Over 200 horses march in this grand parade. These include Drum Horses, a heavy breed that carries a rider and a large set of drums—and is trained to stay steady while the drums are being played!

SWEDISH WARMBLOOD

One of the world's oldest warmblood breeds, this handsome horse has its origins in the 17th century when Dutch, Spanish, and English stallions, among others, were imported to Sweden and bred with local mares. The aim was to create top-notch horses for Swedish soldiers, which were swift and strong enough to cope with the battlefield.

These early horses shared similar characteristics but varied in size and appearance. In the 19th and 20th centuries, Thoroughbreds (p.41), Arabs (p.88), Hanoverians (p.55), and Trakehners (p.70) were brought in to make the breed more powerful. Nowadays, Swedish Warmbloods make outstanding riding and competition horses, which perform especially well in dressage and show jumping.

HORSE PROFILE
Country: Sweden
Type: Light **Height:** 16.2 hands
Colors: Any solid color
Personality: Elegant, agile, fast

FINNISH HORSE

The Finnish Horse (or Finnhorse) is Finland's only horse breed. There were originally two types—the Draft, which was used to transport timber and plow fields, and the Universal, which had a lighter build and was bred for trotting races.

Modern Finn Horses are closer to the Universal in looks but they are still perfectly capable of lending a hoof on the farm when needed. This is a multitalented breed that is prized in Finnish riding schools for its calm nature, agility in the show ring, and ability to pull a sleigh across a snowy plain with ease.

These compact horses are exceptionally strong and can pull up to twice their own weight!

Finnish Horses are used to take tourists on nighttime sleigh rides to see the magical Northern Lights.

HORSE PROFILE
Country: Finland
Type: Light **Height:** 15.1 hands
Colors: Chestnut
Personality: Strong, hardworking, versatile

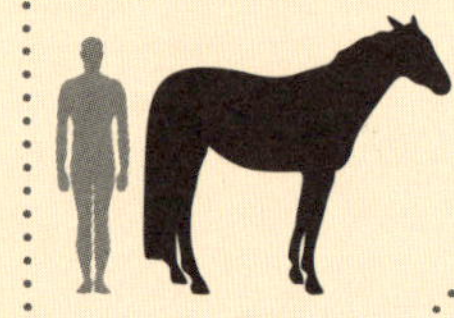

FRIESIAN

Are you looking for Black Beauty? Look no further! The jet-black Friesian is one of Europe's oldest and most iconic breeds. Its ancestors are thought to have been medieval warhorses, which were created by crossing Dutch and Spanish breeds.

Friesians are powerfully built, agile, and friendly, making them excellent all-rounders. Across the centuries, they have been used for farming and riding, and today, they perform well in dressage and harness racing. Because of their smart black coats and sensible nature, Friesians are often used to pull carriages at funerals and other important occasions.

HORSE PROFILE
Country: Netherlands
Type: Light **Height:** 15.3 hands
Colors: Black
Personality: Easygoing, calm, glamorous

Friesians are now bred to be all black. The only marking that is allowed is a white star on the horse's forehead.

BELGIAN WARMBLOOD

The Belgian Warmblood was created between the 1930s and 1950s by crossing Belgian farm horses with a Dutch breed called a Gelderlander. Selle Francais (p.51), Thoroughbreds (p.41), and Holsteiners (p.54) were later added to create a powerful and agile sport horse.

Belgian Warmbloods have muscly legs and strong hindquarters, which makes them perfect for show jumping. A famous Belgian Warmblood called Big Ben won over 40 Grand Prix titles (the highest level of show jumping) during the 1980s and 1990s.

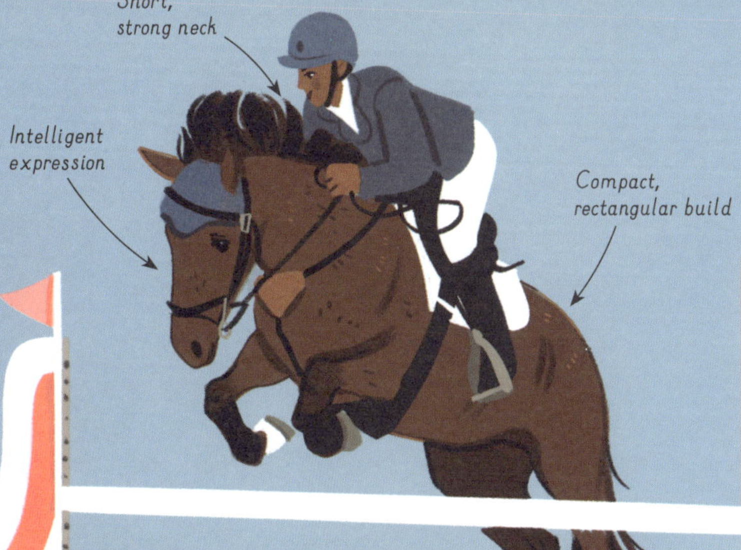

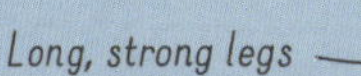

HORSE PROFILE
Country: Belgium
Type: Light **Height:** 16.2 hands
Colors: Any solid color, often bay, chestnut, gray, brown, or black
Personality: Fast, strong, spirited

PERCHERON

Strength, style, and a sweet-nature: the Percheron has it all. Its ancestors are thought to have been large French horses that were crossed with Arabs (p.88) and Spanish breeds in the Middle Ages (c.450–1450). This magical mix created one of the world's best-loved and most adaptable draft breeds.

Over the centuries, Percherons have carried knights into battle, farmed the land, pulled coaches, and hauled machinery. They are traditionally dapple-gray in color—lighter horses were favored by stagecoach drivers as they could be seen on the roads at night. Today, Percherons are used for farmwork as well as appearing in shows and parades. If you visit Disneyland Paris, you might spot one of these dazzling horses pulling Cinderella's carriage!

This horse's mane and tail have been braided with ribbons to stop them from getting tangled.

HORSE PROFILE
Country: France **Type:** Heavy
Height: 16.2 hands
Colors: Traditionally dapple-gray, though can also be black, bay, chestnut, or roan
Personality: Obedient, adaptable, courageous

NORMAN COB

This compact horse comes from the lush pastures of Normandy in northern France. It's descended from a breed called a Carrossier Normand, created in the 17th century by crossing draft horses with lighter breeds, and was prized as a carriage horse.

By the 20th century, the breed had been split into two types—lighter horses for riding and heavier horses (the Norman Cobs) for farmwork. Norman Cobs can still be seen on farms in northern France. They also make excellent horses for vaulting (gymnastics on horseback) due to their broad, strong backs.

HORSE PROFILE
Country: France
Type: Heavy **Height:** 15.3–16.2 hands
Colors: Typically chestnut, bay, or seal brown (brown body with darker legs, mane, and tail)
Personality: Sensible, strong, versatile

Carrossier Normands were used by French mailmen in the 19th century; they had the stamina to pull a cart for hours and the patience to wait quietly while letters were delivered.

This horse is wearing a rosette—a decoration made of ribbons awarded as a prize in horsey sporting events.

Strong hocks help the horse jump

Powerful hindquarters

Strong, elegant neck

Head looks similar to a French Trotter

Hard hooves

SELLE FRANCAIS

During the 19th century, stables throughout France began importing Thoroughbreds (p.41) to breed with their local mares and create elegant riding horses. By the early 20th century, several distinct types had emerged, notably from Normandy and western and eastern France. These crossbreeds were grouped together under one name in 1958—the Selle Francais (or French Saddlehorse).

French Trotters (below) have been used to refine the Selle Francais over the last 70 years and create a nimble horse that excels in show jumping. These sporty horses frequently rank among the world's best jumpers, scooping up medals at Olympic Games and other international championships.

HORSE PROFILE
Country: France **Type:** Light
Height: Usually over 16 hands
Colors: Bay or chestnut
Personality: Athletic, strong, graceful

FRENCH TROTTER

The French Trotter was developed in the early 19th century for a type of horse racing called trotting. During trotting, a horse must perform an unbroken trot, moving its legs in diagonal pairs. The horse either pulls a lightweight cart (called a sulky) while trotting or is ridden by a jockey.

Breeders in Normandy used a wide range of horses to perfect the French Trotter. They crossed local mares with Thoroughbreds (p.41) for stamina and Norfolk Trotters for their trotting skills. American Standardbreds (p.17) were later added for extra speed.

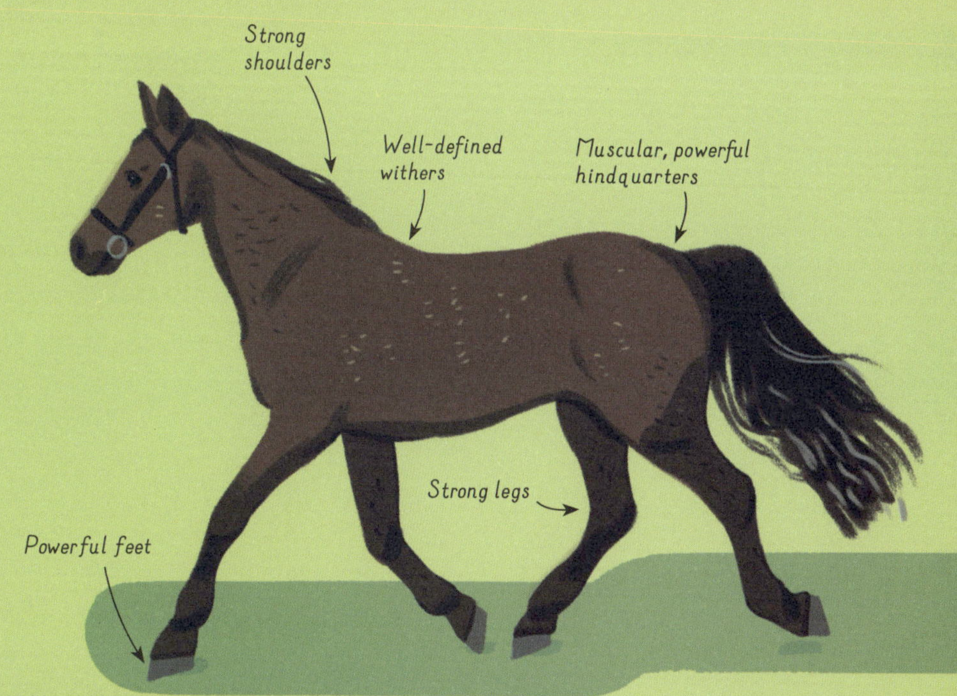

HORSE PROFILE
Country: France
Type: Light **Height:** 16.2 hands
Colors: Chestnut, brown, or bay
Personality: Tough, athletic, focused

ARDENNAIS

The Ardennais is one of the biggest horses on the stable block. This chunky breed is more thickset than any other draft horse, with short, tree-trunk-like legs to maximize its pulling power.

These burly horses come from the Ardennes region, which covers parts of northern France, Belgium, Germany, and Luxembourg. Since ancient times, the horses of this rugged landscape have been admired for their strength and hardiness—the Roman leader Julius Caesar was a fan.

Until the mid-20th century, the Ardennais was mainly a warhorse. These brave horses carried knights in the medieval Crusades (1095–1291), lugged guns to Russia for the French Emperor Napoleon in the 19th century, and hauled supplies in both World Wars. Nowadays, they are used in France for farm and forestry work, such as hauling logs (as shown here).

Despite their tank-like looks, Ardennais are gentle souls and will happily be handled by children. They make wonderful therapy horses due to their calm presence.

Muscular body

Broad, short back

Short, thick legs

Thick feathering around feet

Fairly small feet compared to large body size

HORSE PROFILE
Country: France
Type: Heavy **Height:** Over 17 hands
Colors: Black, brown, bay, or gray
Personality: Loyal, hardworking, kindly

BRETON

This sleek and sturdy horse has its roots in Brittany, a region in northwest France. There are two official versions of the Breton—a lighter type called the Breton Postier and a heavier type called the Breton Heavy Draft (pictured).

Both Bretons are hardworking horses with enormous stamina. The Postier was originally developed for light farmwork and as a military horse, while the Heavy Draft did the tougher lifting and pulling tasks. The Heavy Draft is the more common of the two and is often used on vineyards in the south of France to plow fields and transport boxes of grapes.

HORSE PROFILE
Country: France **Type:** Heavy
Height: 15.1–16 hands
Colors: Usually chestnut with a flaxen mane and tail
Personality: Willing, hardy, friendly

BOULONNAIS

The rare and beautiful Boulonnais comes from the north coast of France. Its ancestors were developed at the time of the medieval Crusades (1095–1291) by crossing local working breeds with lighter German breeds to create strong, nimble warhorses.

In the 17th century, Spanish horses and Arabs (p.88) were added, giving the breed an extra dash of elegance. There are two types of Boulonnais—a lighter type, originally used to transport carts of fish swiftly from seaside towns to Paris, and a heavier type, which did the farmwork.

The Boulonnais is unusually pretty and dainty for a heavy breed.

HORSE PROFILE
Country: France
Type: Heavy **Height:** 15.1–17.3 hands
Colors: Usually gray but can be chestnut or black, too
Personality: Elegant, powerful, energetic

OLDENBURGER

The elegant Oldenburger is named after an ancient region of northwest Germany. It was developed by local aristocrats in the 17th century by crossing Friesians (p.49) with Spanish and Italian horses. These early Oldenburgers were robust but graceful and were used to pull carriages as well as work on farms.

In the 20th century, Thoroughbreds (p.41) were added to transform the breed into a sleek sport horse. Although they are not as fast as German breeds such as the Hanoverian (see opposite), Oldenburgers make stunning show jumping and dressage horses thanks to their powerful build and eager-to-please nature.

HORSE PROFILE
Country: Germany
Type: Light **Height:** 16.2–17.2 hands
Colors: Usually black, brown, or bay
Personality: Strong, obedient, stylish

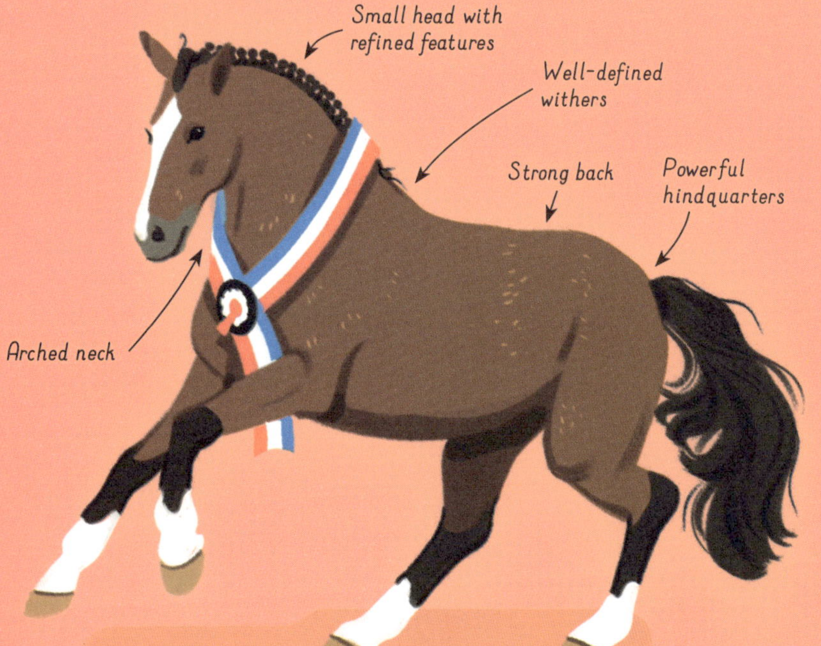

HOLSTEINER

The Holsteiner has had many roles during its 700-year history. Its ancestors were small horses that lived in north Germany, where they were used by monks to ride through misty marshes. These horses were later mixed with Arabs (p.88) and Spanish breeds to produce agile farmworkers. By the 19th century, Holsteiners had been crossed with English coach horses and put to work pulling carriages.

In the 1940s, the Holsteiner was reinvented for the final time. Thoroughbreds (p.41) were added to create horses that were tall, precise, and perfect for show jumping. Ever since, these springy athletes have ruled the world's show jumping scene.

HORSE PROFILE
Country: Germany
Type: Light **Height:** 16–17 hands
Colors: Any solid color, but black, bay, brown, or gray are common
Personality: Bold, good-natured, graceful

HANOVERIAN

This noble-looking horse was developed in the 1730s by George II, the king of Great Britain, who set up a famous stable near his home city of Hanover in Germany. There, local horses were crossed with German, English, Italian, and Spanish breeds to create the Hanoverian.

Hanoverians were originally used to pull coaches, carry soldiers, and, sometimes, double-up as farm horses. In the 1940s, Trakehners (p.70) and Thoroughbreds (p.41) were introduced to turn the breed into a sport horse. Today, these stately horses excel at dressage, show jumping, and eventing.

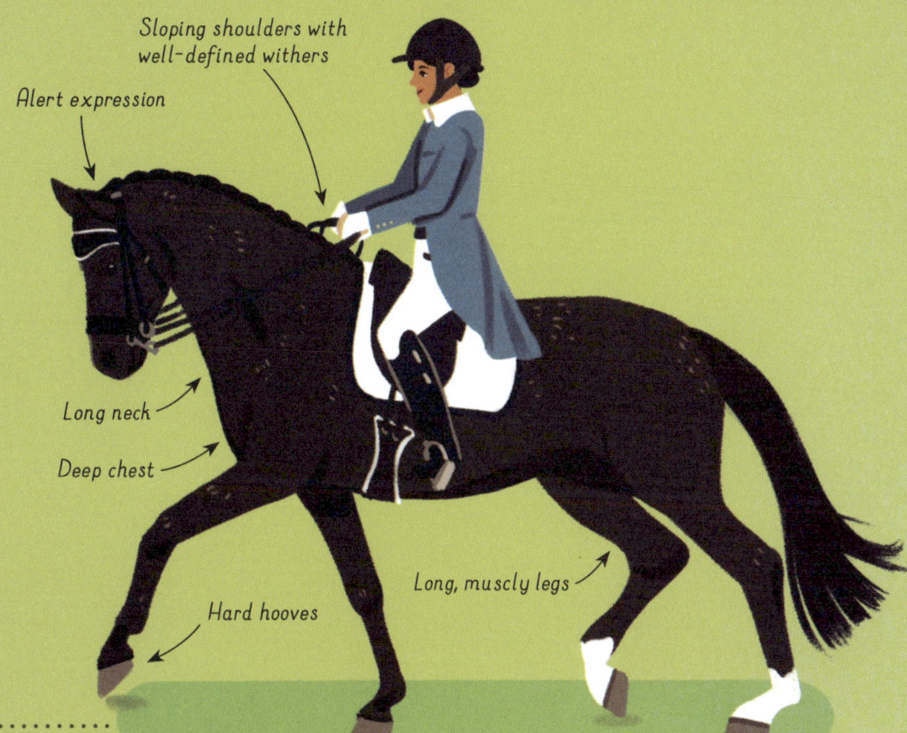

HORSE PROFILE
Country: Germany
Type: Light **Height:** 15.3–17.1 hands
Colors: Any solid color, but black, bay, chestnut, or gray are common
Personality: Calm, athletic, elegant

HAFLINGER

Are you planning a trek up a mountain? Then take a Haflinger with you! These small horses come from the Tyrolean Mountains between Austria and Italy. There, they work on farms, lug logs through forests, and help travelers navigate treacherous paths. Strong and remarkably sure-footed, the Haflinger is the ultimate mountaineering buddy.

The breed was officially established in the 1870s, when a local mare bred with an Arab (p.88) stallion. Their stunning golden foal (called Folie) became the founding father of the modern Haflinger breed. Nowadays, Haflingers are popular around the world for trail riding and dressage, and make top therapy horses because of their steady and extremely kind characters.

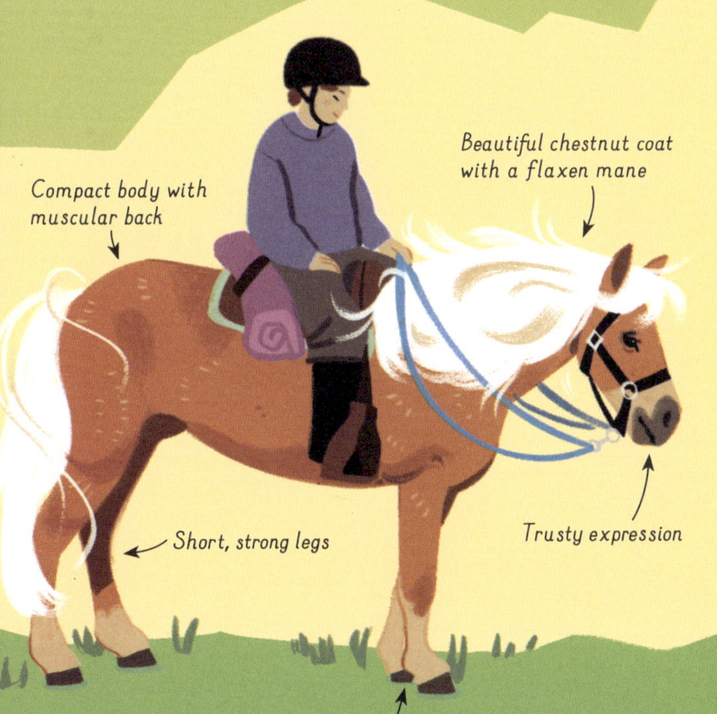

HORSE PROFILE
Country: Austria
Type: Light **Height:** 13.2–15 hands
Colors: Chestnut
Personality: Reliable, gentle, intelligent

FREE-ROAMING HORSES

While most domestic horses live and work alongside people, some trot a wilder path. Domestic horses that live in the wild with little human contact are known as feral horses. Domestic horses that are left to roam freely in the wild but have an owner are called semi-feral horses. Herds of feral and semi-feral horses are found in many parts of the world, and they have often adapted to survive in unique environments. Here are just a few of the planet's free-roaming breeds.

MUSTANG (USA)

Nothing conjures up the spirit of the American West like the sight of a herd of Mustangs galloping across a wide, open plain. These feral horses have dashed across the deserts and prairies of the USA since the 17th century, when Spanish and other European settlers turned their spare horses loose.

Today, there are around 86,000 Mustangs in America. Because they have bred freely with one another, they come in a range of colors and sizes (although most are between 14–15 hands high). They are fast, hardy, and healthy horses and can be tamed for leisure riding and ranch work.

CHINCOTEAGUE (USA)

Despite being named after Chincoteague Island on America's East Coast, these ponies live on neighboring Assateague Island. Legend tells how a Spanish ship was wrecked there in the 17th century and a herd of plucky ponies swam to shore. In reality, their ancestors were probably abandoned there by settlers.

Chincoteague ponies eat tough beach grasses and seaweeds, which are high in salt. Because of this, they drink twice as much water as other horses, meaning their tummies look bloated. This doesn't affect their health or agility; each year, they are rounded up and swim to Chincoteague so they can be checked over by a vet.

CAMARGUE (FRANCE)

A wetland in the south of France is the stomping ground of a very special group of horses. Camargues are descended from prehistoric equines and are thought to have been influenced by Spanish, Arabian, and African breeds over the last 3,000 years. These robust horses have large hooves that are flatter and more water-resistant than other breeds and an ability to survive on chewy marshland plants. Camargues love being in water and can often be seen splashing through the lagoons. Although many Camargues live a wild existence, some have been tamed by local farmers, called *gardians*, who use them to round up their black cattle that graze on the marshes.

Dartmoor Pony

Exmoor Pony

EXMOOR AND DARTMOOR PONIES (UK)

It is believed that the Exmoor pony has its roots in ancient ponies that were domesticated by the Celts (c.400 BCE). The first record of ponies on Exmoor, a remote moor in Devon, England, dates from 1086.

Many are now kept as pets, but some still live semi-feral on the moor. These tough ponies are perfectly adapted to life in a cold climate. They grow a woolly, double-coat in winter, have a fan of thick hairs at the top of their tail (called a "snow chute") to deflect water, and fleshy rims around their eyes (called "toad" eye) to keep the rain out.

The Dartmoor is another beautiful semi-feral pony that can still be found roaming the valleys and hills of its windswept Devon home. Like the Exmoor, its ancestors were ponies domesticated by ancient Britons. However, over the years, Dartmoors have been used widely as riding ponies and mining ponies and crossed with other breeds (such as Welsh Ponies).

Feral and semi-feral horses live freely in herds, usually made up of a stallion, mares, and their foals. These horses find their own food and shelter rather than rely on people to look after them. Other feral and semi-feral horses include the Icelandic (p.44), Brumby (p.106), and Skyrian (p.65).

EUROPE (South & East)

Welcome to a land where horsey worlds collide. Many horses and ponies in southern and eastern Europe share histories with their cousins in the north of the continent, but they also reflect the influence of Asian and African breeds. As a result, this part of Europe is home to some of the world's most exciting and extravagant horses. In this chapter, we'll meet spectacular show jumpers like Italy's Salerno, graceful carriage horses like Czechia's Kladruber, and perhaps the most breathtaking breed of all—Slovenia's dancing Lipizzaner.

Sorraia horses are currently being used in rewilding projects in Portugal. Through their grazing, the horses help to maintain natural habitats and help other wildlife thrive.

Thanks to their glamorous looks and intelligence, Andalusians are often used for film work. Two Andalusian stallions called Domero and Blanco starred as the magical Shadowfax in the Lord of the Rings films.

Chariot racing was a popular sport in ancient Greece. Riders would perch on a small chariot pulled by teams of horses. In one type of chariot racing, riders had to jump out of their moving chariot, run beside it, and then jump back in!

Each spring, the city of Jerez in Andalusia hosts a festival that celebrates horses. People in traditional Spanish dress parade through the city streets with their Andalusians, as shown here.

ANDALUSIAN

Twenty thousand years ago in what is now Spain, a prehistoric person picked up a brush and carefully painted a horse onto the wall of a cave. That horse was a distant ancestor of today's Andalusian.

The breed was developed from the 15th century, when Spanish royals set up stables in Andalusia, in southern Spain. Many of these stables were run by monks, who left written records of the breed's development. Local horses were bred with Barbs (p.76) from North Africa to create beautiful equines for Spanish kings, queens, and armies to ride.

Andalusians were given as gifts to other European aristocrats, helping the breed to become popular outside of Spain. Their strong presence and proud way of walking makes them ideal for classical dressage (called *haute école*), as well as stunning riding horses.

HORSE PROFILE
Country: Spain
Type: Light **Height:** 15–15.2 hands
Colors: Usually gray or bay, but can come in other colors, such as black, palomino, or chestnut
Personality: Intelligent, strong, beautiful

LUSITANO

The Lusitano is a close cousin of the Andalusian (see opposite) and shares its ancient roots. In fact, the horses were considered one breed until the 1960s.

Historically, Lusitanos were used as warhorses and for general riding, driving, and classical dressage—where horses perform a series of elaborate jumps, hops, and dances. Specialized schools, such as the Portuguese School of Equestrian Art in Lisbon, the country's capital city, still put on classical dressage performances using Lusitanos.

HORSE PROFILE

Country: Portugal
Type: Light **Height:** 15–16 hands
Colors: Usually gray or bay
Personality: Affectionate, hardworking, graceful

SORRAIA

The sturdy Sorraia is one of the world's rarest and most endangered breeds. These little horses are named after the Sorraia River in Portugal, where a zoologist found a herd in the 1920s.

The Sorraia are thought to have lived wild on the plains and marshes along the river for thousands of years, although local people would occasionally tame them and use them for cattle herding and farmwork. Today, there are only around 200 Sorraia left and they live in protected herds.

HORSE PROFILE

Country: Portugal
Type: Light **Height:** 14.1–14.3 hands
Colors: Usually dun
Personality: Independent, tough, agile

ITALIAN HEAVY DRAFT

The Italian Heavy Draft comes from the wide plains of northern Italy. It was developed in the second half of the 19th century by farmers who needed strong but quick-moving horses to help them in the fields. They crossed local mares with various European heavy breeds—notably Bretons (p.53)—to create their perfect horse.

Italian Heavy Drafts are prized for their speediness, even when pulling heavy loads. In Italy, they are also called the Tiro Pesante Rapido, which means "fast farm horse."

HORSE PROFILE
Country: Italy
Type: Heavy **Height:** 15–16 hands
Colors: Usually chestnut
Personality: Gentle, strong, fast

MAREMMANO

This rustic breed comes from the Maremma region on the west coast of Italy. Renowned for their cattle skills, these horses have helped Italian cowboys (called *butteri*) round up livestock in the area's hills and marshlands for centuries. Today, *butteri* still use Maremmanos to round up long-horned cattle in the Maremma National Park.

Many breeds are thought to have been used to develop the Maremmano, including Spanish, Neapolitan, Thoroughbred (p.41), Arab (p.88), and Barb (p.76). Maremmanos are not very quick, but they make great riding buddies and police horses due to their strength and willing natures.

HORSE PROFILE
Country: Italy
Type: Light **Height:** 15.3 hands
Colors: Any solid color, but usually bay, brown, black, or chestnut
Personality: Hardworking, calm, tough

SALERNO

This athletic horse comes from the southwest of Italy and evolved from a now-extinct breed called a Neapolitan. The Neapolitan developed around the city of Naples between the 16th and 19th centuries and was one of the finest riding horses of its time. These horses were mixed with Spanish, Arab (p.88), Barb (p.76), and, later, Thoroughbreds (p.41) to create the sleek and speedy Salerno.

Salernos are rare today, but they used to be popular show jumping horses. A famous Italian rider called Raimondo d'Inzeo won a gold medal at the 1960 Olympic Games riding a Salerno called Posillipo.

Strong, sloping shoulders

Short, strong back

Elegant head reflects Spanish heritage

Powerful hindquarters

Slender legs

HORSE PROFILE
Country: Italy
Type: Light **Height:** 16 hands
Colors: Usually black, bay, or chestnut
Personality: Sensible, gentle, agile

MURGESE

The impressive Murgese comes from the wooded hills and dry plateaus of Puglia in southeast Italy. Its ancestors were ridden by Italian soldiers in the 15th and 16th centuries, but then the breed declined. Fans of the Murgese started a breeding program in the 1920s to save the breed and find it a new job as a light draft horse on farms.

Murgese are still used for farmwork in Puglia, as well as for trekking and cross-country riding. They are also often crossed with donkeys to produce strong mules.

HORSE PROFILE
Country: Italy
Type: Light **Height:** 15–16 hands
Colors: Usually black or blue roan
Personality: Hardy, active, even-tempered

LIPIZZANER

No horse combines style and skill quite like the Lipizzaner. These dreamy horses are famous for their spectacular dance shows at the Spanish Riding School in Vienna, Austria. For over 450 years, the school has specialized in a type of classical dressage called *haute école* (high school). During performances, a fleet of sparkling-white Lipizzaners display breathtaking leaps, jumps, and moves to music.

Although the horses are associated with Vienna, the Lipizzaner originated in the mountain village of Lipica in Slovenia. The breed was developed there in the 16th and 17th centuries, when classical riding schools became fashionable across Europe. Breeders used a mix of Spanish horses, Barbs (p.76), Arabs (p.88), and Neapolitans to create these magical, nimble-hoofed horses.

Low withers

Silky mane and tail

Elegant head

Muscular, compact body

Strong, hard feet

This Lipizzaner is putting on an acrobatic show. When not performing, the horses are cared for in the Spanish Riding School's stables. In the summer, they take breaks from training at special riding centers in the Austrian countryside.

HORSE PROFILE

Country: Slovenia **Type:** Light
Height: 14.2–15.2 hands
Colors: Gray-white
Personality: Elegant, athletic, intelligent

Traditionally, only Lipizzaner stallions perform at the Spanish School. It takes about six years for a Lipizzaner to complete its training, which is gentle and guided by what the horse feels comfortable with. A small number of talented stallions are taught the most difficult moves, in which all four of the horse's feet leave the floor (called "airs above the ground").

PINDOS

These tough ponies come from the rugged Pindus Mountains in northern Greece. For centuries, they have been used by local farmers for plowing, lugging timber, and pack work, as well as for general riding. They are also bred with donkeys to create strong mules.

Their origins are uncertain but it's thought they may have some Asian heritage. Pindos are perfectly adapted to their mountain home, with hard, nimble hooves for clambering over rocks, incredible endurance, and an ability to survive on minimal food when times are tough.

HORSE PROFILE

Country: Greece
Type: Pony **Height:** 12 hands
Colors: Typically bay, black, or gray
Personality: Strong, stubborn, hardy

SKYRIAN

Meet the small but mighty Skyrian. It's thought these little horses were once found across ancient Greece (1200–323 BCE). Legend tells how they pulled the chariot of the hero Achilles, and equines that look like Skyrians are carved into the marble that decorate a famous ancient temple, the Parthenon, in Athens.

Today, only around 200 of these very rare horses remain on the Greek island of Skyros. To help protect them, conservation teams have started a breeding program and are training them for activities such as riding and therapy projects.

HORSE PROFILE

Country: Greece
Type: Pony **Height:** 10 hands
Colors: Any solid color, usually bay, dun, black, or dark brown
Personality: Friendly, tough, clever

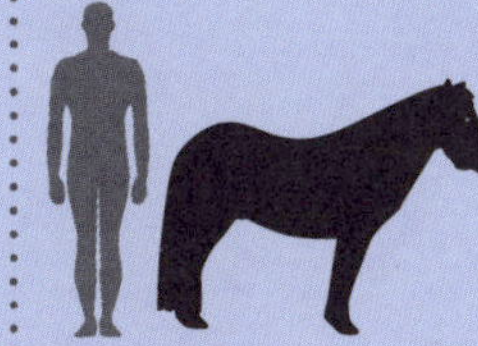

It's thought that the Skyrians' ancestors were normal-sized—they became smaller over hundreds of years to adapt to the island's rugged environment.

SHAGYA-ARABIAN

In the 9th century, an ancient tribe of skilled horse-people began living in the plains and mountains of Hungary in Central Europe. Ever since, Hungary has cherished its deep connection with horses. In the 18th and 19th centuries, the country's breeds were admired across Europe, and the Shagya-Arabian was considered a particular treasure.

The breed is named after Shagya, an Arab stallion bought by the Hungarian king in the 1830s and raised by the Bani Sakher people in the Syrian Desert. All of today's Shagya-Arabians can trace their roots back to him.

Large, expressive eyes

Dipped (or "dished") face

Broad, muscly chest

Similar build to an Arab horse but taller

High-set tail

This classy horse was developed at Babolna, a royal stud farm, in the 1780s by crossing Arab (p.88) stallions with heavier, Hungarian mares. The aim was to create a practical version of the Arab that could carry soldiers into battle and pull carriages with ease and elegance.

The features that made the breed such a good cavalry and carriage horse 200 years ago make it a superb sport horse today. Combining stamina, presence, and speed, Shagya-Arabians are particularly well-suited to dressage, endurance riding, and jumping.

HORSE PROFILE

Country: Hungary
Type: Light **Height:** 15–16 hands
Colors: Usually gray, but can also be bay, chestnut, black, or roan
Personality: Elegant, tough, fast

NONIUS

The noble Nonius was developed in a famous royal stud farm in Mezőhegyes, Hungary, in the 1780s. A stallion called Nonius was brought from Normandy and bred with Arab (p.88), Thoroughbred (p.41), Lipizzaner (p.64), and Spanish horses to establish the breed.

Developed as military mounts, Nonius horses were used for farmwork into the 20th century. They can still sometimes be seen pulling plows on Hungary's great plains, as shown in the top right image. They also make good horses for leisure riding. But these horses are rare, with only around 500 alive today.

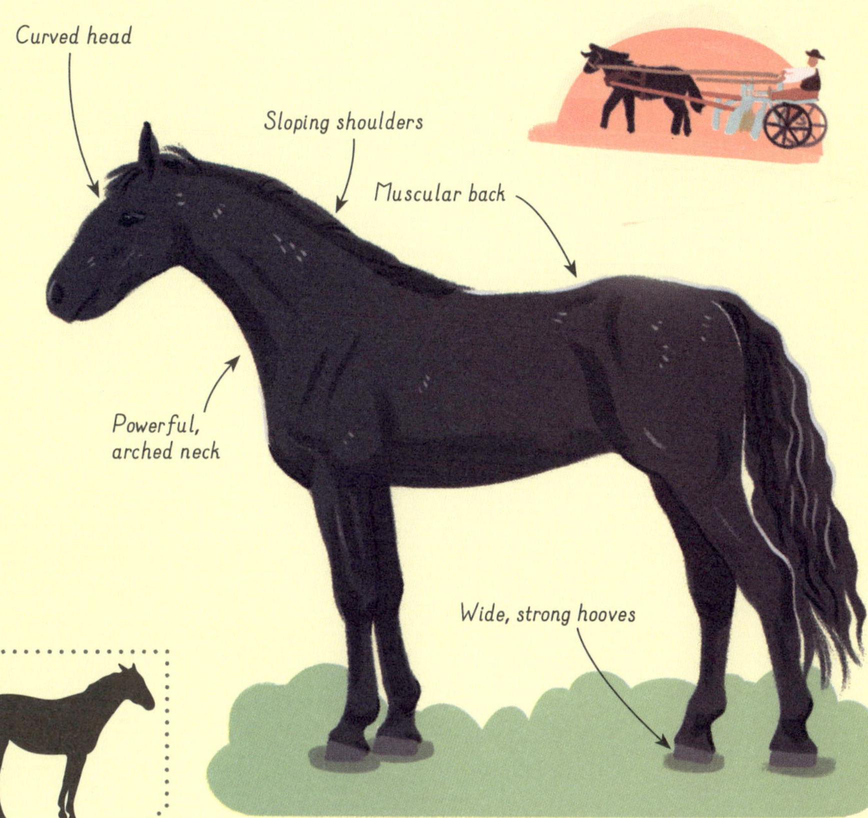

HORSE PROFILE

Country: Hungary
Type: Light **Height:** 15.1–16.1 hands
Colors: Black, brown, or dark bay
Personality: Strong, hardworking, gentle

HUCUL

The name Hucul comes from a Romanian word meaning "rebel" or "outlaw," and it reflects this pony's tough personality. An ancient breed, Huculs are descended from a prehistoric horse called a Tarpan and have been galloping around the Carpathian Mountains in Central Europe for hundreds of years.

In that time, Huculs have been used to pull carts, transport goods over the mountains, haul timber in forests, work on hilltop farms, and carry soldiers.

HORSE PROFILE

Country: Hungary, Slovakia, Czechia, Ukraine, Poland, and Romania
Type: Pony **Height:** 13–14 hands
Colors: Usually bay, dun, black, or chestnut
Personality: Hardy, calm, sure-footed

MYTHICAL HORSES

Horses have galloped into our imaginations and trotted into our folk tales for thousands of years. In some myths, horses are symbols of beauty or bravery; in others, they possess otherworldly powers. Each story reflects our fascination and deep bond with these amazing animals.

MAGICAL UNICORNS

The unicorn is the most famous magical horsey creature of all. In Europe, unicorn myths can be traced back to an ancient Greek historian called Ctesias (c.400 BCE), who wrote about an animal with a pearl-white body and a horn with healing powers.

Ctesias was probably describing a rhinoceros, but the image endured and spread throughout Western culture. In medieval Europe (c.400–1400 CE), many people believed that unicorns were real. Artworks of the time depict huntsmen battling through dark forests to find these enchanting equines.

THE MYSTERIOUS QILIN

A similar myth appeared in ancient China around 2700 BCE. The Chinese version of the unicorn is called the *qilin* ("chee-lin"). It has a horse-like body, a dragon head, a coat covered in scales, and a single horn. Like the European unicorn, the *qilin* is a gentle, wise, and shy creature.

In medieval Europe, people would pay a lot of money for special cups that were said to be made from unicorn horn, which was thought to protect the drinker from poisons. These cups were actually made from the tusks of real-life animals such as rhinos or narwhals.

FLYING FREE

Hot on the hooves of the unicorn is another iconic magical horse—Pegasus. In ancient Greek mythology, Pegasus is born from the blood of Medusa, a monster with snakes for hair. Pegasus is later tamed by a Greek hero, named Bellerophon, and the pair go on many adventures together.

Pegasus is one of many winged horses found in myths around the world. The Turkic cultures of Western and Central Asia, for example, celebrate a flying horse called Tulpar, who represents speed, strength, and freedom. In East Asia, the *qianlima* is a magical horse that can travel 1,000 Chinese miles (500 km) in a single day thanks to its powerful wings.

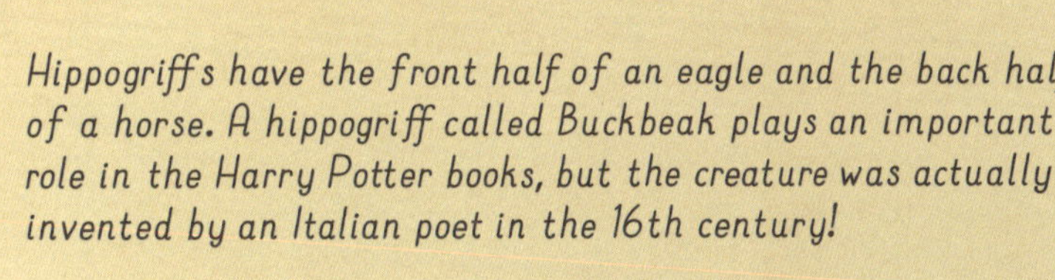

Hippogriffs have the front half of an eagle and the back half of a horse. A hippogriff called Buckbeak plays an important role in the Harry Potter books, but the creature was actually invented by an Italian poet in the 16th century!

CUNNING KELPIES

Some horse stories have a darker side. The kelpie is a shape-shifting water spirit from Scottish folklore. Kelpies are said to live in lakes and rivers where they take the form of beautiful horses that lure travelers to their doom.

As soon as a human sits on a kelpie, they are trapped by the horse's sticky coat and carried off into the water to be eaten! The good news is that kelpies have a weak spot—their bridle. If you can keep hold of a kelpie's bridle, you can control the horse and escape.

UKRAINIAN SADDLE HORSE

This strong horse was developed after World War II in the region of Dnipro in central Ukraine. Breeders crossed Hungarian mares with Trakehners (see below), Hanoverians (p.55), and Thoroughbreds (p.41). A few stud farms also used a now-extinct breed called a Russian Saddle Horse —any Ukrainian Saddle Horse with this heritage is considered particularly special.

Ukrainian Saddle Horses have appeared at Olympic Games and World and European Championships. As well as being nimble dressage and show jumping horses, they make friendly riding horses.

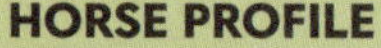

HORSE PROFILE

Country: Ukraine **Type:** Light
Height: 15.7–16.2 hands
Colors: Usually bay, brown, or chestnut
Personality: Calm, well-behaved, powerful

TRAKEHNER

This breed is named after the town of Trakehen in modern-day Russia. It was developed in the 18th century, when the town was part of East Prussia (now split between Russia, Lithuania, and Poland).

Local Lithuanian horses, which were renowned for their hardiness and intelligence, were crossed with sporty breeds, such as Thoroughbreds (p.41) and Arabs (p.88). Originally used to pull coaches and carry soldiers, today the Trakehner is a fantastic jumper and dressage horse. Its springy way of walking makes it look especially elegant in the show ring.

HORSE PROFILE

Country: Lithuania and Russia
Type: Light **Height:** 15.2–17 hands
Colors: Any solid color, usually chestnut, bay, black, or gray
Personality: Spirited, strong, graceful

WIELKOPOLSKI

Named after a region in west-central Poland, the Wielkopolski (you say it "ve-el-ko-pol-ski") is a fairly modern breed. It was developed in 1964 by crossing two now-extinct Polish breeds—the Poznan, a heavier farm horse, and the Mazury, a lighter riding horse closely related to the Trakehner (see opposite).

There are two distinct types of Wielkopolskis. The most popular version is a light, athletic horse used for dressage and show jumping. The other is a heavier type, bred for driving and general riding.

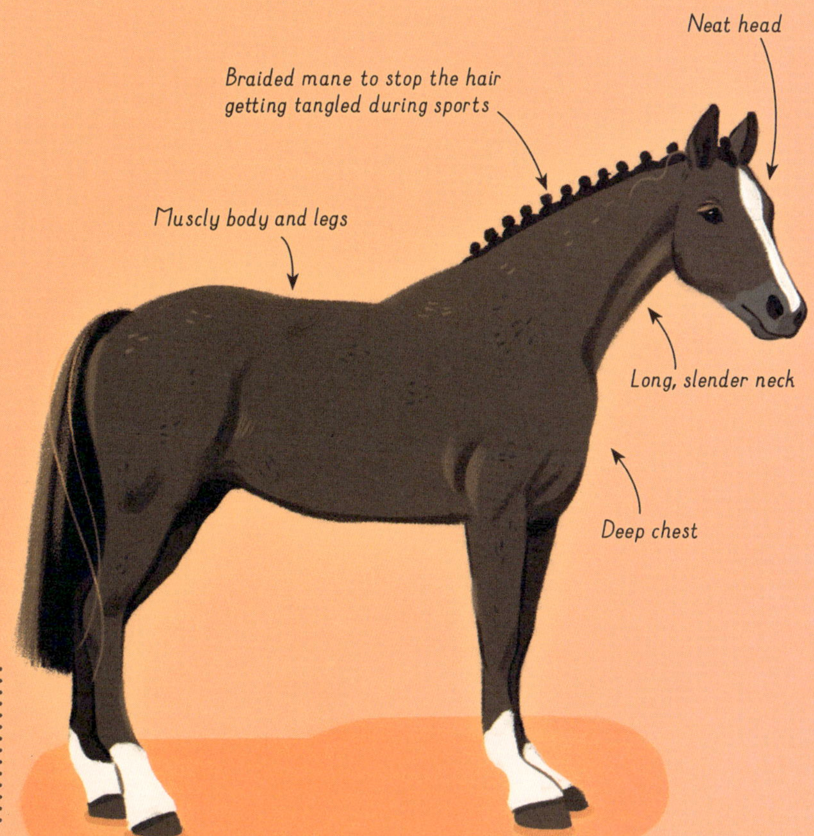

HORSE PROFILE
Country: Poland
Type: Light **Height:** 15.2–16.2 hands
Colors: Gray, bay, chestnut, or black
Personality: Hardy, calm, elegant

KLADRUBER

The Kladruber was created for a very special purpose—to pull carriages for kings and queens. This rare breed can be traced to the 16th century, when a stud farm was set up in the town of Kladruby in Czechia for the Habsburg monarchy (the royal family who ruled much of Europe at the time).

Kladrubers come in only two colors—gray horses were traditionally used to pull royal carriages, while black horses were used for important religious people and at funerals. Today, these stately equines are used as police and riding horses in Czechia.

Curved head (called a Roman nose)
Arched, elegant neck
Upright shoulders
Large, bright eyes
Deep chest
Strong legs

There is no longer a monarchy in Czechia, but Kladrubers are still used to pull carriages by the Danish and Swedish royal families.

HORSE PROFILE
Country: Czechia
Body type: Light **Height:** 15.3–17 hands
Colors: Gray or black
Personality: Noble, calm, strong

HORSE SPORTS

Taking part in a sporty activity with a horse is a great way to build your bond. Whether you just want to have fun or have your eyes set on Olympic Gold, your top priority should always be the welfare of your equine pal. As long as horses are healthy and happy to get involved, they can try all sorts of amazing activities.

SHOW JUMPING AND CROSS-COUNTRY

In show jumping, a horse carries its rider through a course of fences, usually in a time limit. Fences can include upright jumps, crossed poles, and spread fences (wider jumps made up of multiple poles). Show jumping horses need to be powerful and precise. Breeds such as the Selle Francais (p.51), Holsteiner (p.54), and Dutch Warmblood are especially good at it.

If you want a jumping event that's a bit more outdoorsy, try cross-country. This exciting competition takes horses and their riders through a course of natural-looking obstacles, such as log jumps, hedges, and ponds.

Eventing is the horsey version of a triathlon. Over the course of several days, horses and their riders take part in three events—dressage, show jumping, and cross-country.

DRESSAGE

In dressage, a horse is trained to perform a series of delicate movements, such as pirouettes, loops, and elegant trots. Spanish and Portuguese horses and warmblood breeds are traditionally used for dressage, but all horses can try their hoof at it. In recent years, heavier horses and ponies have become popular in the dressage ring.

COMBINED DRIVING

In this event, either a single horse, a pair of horses, or a team of four pulls a light carriage or cart. There are three parts to a combined driving competition: dressage, when particular movements have to be performed; marathon, when the carriage is pulled around a course featuring tunnels, turns, and hills; and obstacle driving, when the rider must guide the horses through a narrow set of cones.

Good dressage is all about the close bond between the horse and rider. The FEI, the international organization that oversees horse sports, sets rules to ensure that horses are well cared for in training and competitions.

FUN AND GAMES

Want to try something a little more unusual? If you like basketball, give horseball a go—it's a game where teams of players throw a ball to one another while riding horses. Or if gymnastics is more your thing, check out vaulting, a sport where riders perform acrobatics on horseback.

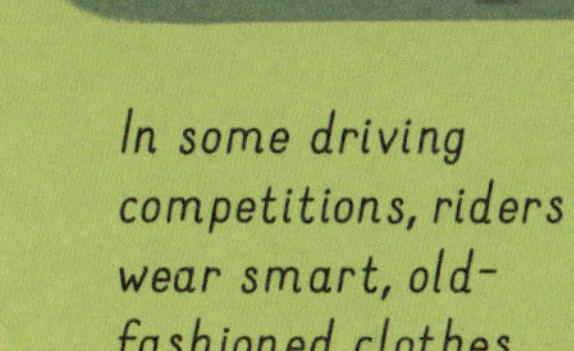

In some driving competitions, riders wear smart, old-fashioned clothes.

HORSE RACING

Horse racing is one of the most recognizable horse sports but it raises animal welfare issues. Many horses can experience injury and distress during racing. Horse racing is split into three main categories—flat racing, jump racing, and harness racing. In flat racing, a horse sprints around a racetrack, while harness racing involves a horse running while pulling a buggy. Jump races, such as hurdles and steeplechases, feature obstacles.

The Barb is named after the region of North Africa where the breed was originally developed. This area used to be called the Barbary Coast.
BARB
MOROCCO, ALGERIA, TUNISIA
M'BAYAR
SENEGAL
Bhirum ponies are well adapted to the warm, dry deserts and plains of Northern Nigeria and are used to carrying goods and doing farmwork in the heat.
DONGOLA
SUDAN, CAMEROON, ERITREA
FLEUVE
SENEGAL
BHIRUM
NIGERIA
Known for their fearlessness and stamina, the Basuto was one of many horse and pony breeds used in the Second Boer War (1899–1902), a battle fought between the British Army and the Boers (descendants of Dutch settlers) in South Africa.

HORSE CULTURE

Horses play a special role in many African cultures. The Hausa people of West Africa, for example, celebrate them in their Kilisa Festival, during which horses wear decorative bridles and saddles and take part in riding displays.

The Mossi people of Burkina Faso also have an ancient tradition of horsemanship. According to legend, the Mossi kingdom was founded by Princess Yennenga, shown above, who ran away from her father's lands on a white horse. She and her son, Ouedraogo (which means "stallion"), ruled over the Mossi empire. Horseback riding and horse racing remain an important part of Burkina Faso's culture to this day.

AFRICA

Africa is a continent where speedy stallions thunder over deserts, nimble ponies hike up enormous mountains, and hardy horses carry riders across wide savannas. Bred to cope with some of the planet's most extreme climates, Africa's horses are a strong and special herd. The north of Africa is the kingdom of the Barb, an old breed that has influenced many of the continent's home-grown horses, while to the west and east, we meet rare equines, such as the Dongola and M'Bayar. In contrast, the horses in the south reflect the influence of Dutch settlers and the European and Asian breeds they brought with them from the 17th century onward.

Horses were introduced to Egypt in around 1700–1550 BCE. The ancient Egyptians viewed horses as symbols of power—they were used to pull the chariots of pharaohs in peacetime and military figures during battles. Some horses were even mummified and buried alongside their royal owners.

BARB

Barbs have been kicking up dust in the North African desert for thousands of years. These speedy horses are riding buddies of the Berber people, the original inhabitants of Morocco, Algeria, and Tunisia.

Barbs still play an important role in Berber culture. The horses are used in a dramatic performance called a "Fantasia," shown here, which celebrates the relationship between horse and rider. During a Fantasia, teams race across the desert before firing an old-fashioned musket (a type of gun) into the air. The team whose performance is the most in sync wins a prize.

Barbs have influenced some of the world's most iconic breeds. When North African armies traveled to Spain in 711 CE, they were accompanied by their trusty Barbs. Spanish breeders admired the power and hardiness of these warhorses and used them to create the Andalusian (p.60). Later, Barbs played a role in the development of the Thoroughbred (p.41), American Quarter Horse (p.20), and Argentine Criollo (p.30), to name a few.

HORSE PROFILE

Country: Morocco, Tunisia, and Algeria
Type: Light **Height:** 14.2–15.2 hands
Colors: Gray, bay, chestnut, or black
Personality: Tough, agile, gentle

Barbs are distantly related to, and often compared with, Arabs (p.88). Like Arabs, Barbs are tough and fast, but they look less elegant and more rustic.

DONGOLA

This rare breed is named after the Dongola region of Sudan but it is found in many other West and East African countries, too. Its history is uncertain, but it may have Barb (see opposite), Arab (p.88), and Spanish ancestry. As there are no official breeding programs for Dongolas, the look and size of these horses varies between countries.

The Dongola has a particularly special relationship with the Fulani people of Cameroon. The Fulani cherish their horses, and Dongolas appear in parades and ceremonies, as well as being used for general riding.

HORSE PROFILE
Country: Sudan, Cameroon, and Eritrea **Type:** Light
Height: 15–15.2 hands
Colors: Black, chestnut, or bay
Personality: Energetic, spirited, strong

BHIRUM

This handsome pony was developed in the north of Nigeria in West Africa. Bhirums are thought to be related to Barbs (see opposite) and a very rare (possibly extinct) Cameroonian breed called the Poney Mousseye.

These little horses have tough, quiet personalities—they don't neigh very much, preferring to get on calmly with their work. In Nigeria, Bhirum ponies are used for light draft and pack jobs, as well as for general riding.

HORSE PROFILE
Country: Nigeria
Type: Pony **Height:** 14–14.2 hands
Colors: Various solid colors, including black, bay, chestnut, or gray
Personality: Reliable, gentle, hardworking

M'BAYAR

The M'Bayar is a sturdy pony that is thought to have been developed from the Barb (p.76) in the region of Baol in central Senegal. In ancient times, this area was renowned for its strong, speedy horses, which were traded with neighboring kingdoms. The M'Bayar is especially prized for its adaptable and willing temperament.

HORSE PROFILE
Country: Senegal
Type: Pony **Height:** 13–14 hands
Colors: Usually bay or chestnut
Personality: Calm, strong, hardworking

Horses and ponies play an essential role in Senegalese life. Millions of people in Senegal rely on equines like M'Bayars, to help them farm the land and for transportation.

FLEUVE

The exact origins of this slender breed are unknown, but it's thought the Fleuve was created by crossing Barbs (p.76) with local ponies. Its name comes from the French word for "river" and it suits this breed well—like a river, Fleuves are swift and powerful.

Fleuves used to belong to Senegalese chieftains. Today, they are used for riding and horse racing, which is a popular sport in Senegal.

HORSE PROFILE
Country: Senegal **Type:** Light
Height: Usually around 14 hands
Colors: Often gray, but can be brown or bay
Personality: Energetic, speedy, hardy

BASUTO

The Basuto has its roots in Arab (p.88) and Middle Eastern horses that were brought to South Africa in the 1650s by Dutch settlers (called Boers). These horses were used to create two breeds—the larger Cape Horse and the smaller, stockier Basuto. The Cape Horse is now extinct, but the Basuto has survived.

Basutos were developed by Dutch breeders in the mountains of South Africa and Lesotho. These sure-footed ponies are fantastic climbers, and are used to carrying farmers and tourists over steep, rocky terrain. Thanks to their long strides, they are very comfortable to ride.

HORSE PROFILE

Country: Lesotho and South Africa
Type: Pony **Height:** 14.2 hands
Colors: Chestnut, gray, brown, black, or bay
Personality: Hardy, courageous, friendly

BOERPERD

The Boerperd is a descendant of the Cape Horse (see above) and was named after the Dutch settlers who developed it in the 19th century. They mixed Cape Horses with British breeds, including Thoroughbreds (p.41), Cleveland Bays, and Hackneys (p.41), to create tough horses with great stamina and speed.

Boerperds were used as warhorses in the Second Boer War (1899–1902) and the breed almost died out as a result. Six herds survived and were used to redevelop the breed between the 1940s and 1990s. Today, Boerperds are used for sports such as eventing and dressage, and for horseback riding safari vacations in South Africa.

HORSE PROFILE

Country: South Africa
Type: Light **Height:** 14–16 hands
Colors: Various colors, including black, dun, chestnut, palomino, or pinto
Personality: Strong, trustworthy, brave

WILD HORSES

All of the horse breeds in this book belong to one species, *Equus caballus,* or the domestic horse. But there are seven other species of horses living in the world today. One of these is the domestic donkey (pp.34–35). The other six live in the wild. Let's meet them!

African wild asses are divided into two subspecies—the Nubian wild ass and the Somali wild ass. You can tell them apart because the Somali wild ass has zebra-like stripes on its legs.

ZEBRAS

There are three species of zebras: the mountain zebra, the plains zebra, and the Grévy's zebra. They are found in savanna, scrubland, and mountainous regions in eastern and southern Africa. Plains and mountain zebras live in family groups called harems, led by a dominant male, while Grévy's zebras usually live alone or in loose herds.

Every individual zebra has a pattern of stripes that is completely unique—just like your fingerprints are to you. Scientists think that a zebra's stripes may help to deter horseflies, which can spread disease among horses. It's thought that the stripes confuse the flies, preventing them from biting the zebra.

AFRICAN WILD ASS

Found in the deserts and grasslands of Eritrea, Ethiopia, and Somalia, the African wild ass is a critically endangered member of the horse family. There are thought to be fewer than 600 alive in the wild today.

This tough equine is the ancestor of the domestic donkey, and the two species look very similar. Like donkeys, African wild asses have big ears, a stiff mane, and a tufted tail. They also make a loud hee-haw sound, which travels easily across the open desert when the animals need to communicate with each other. Although females and their young sometimes form herds, African wild asses live alone or in casual groups for most of their lives.

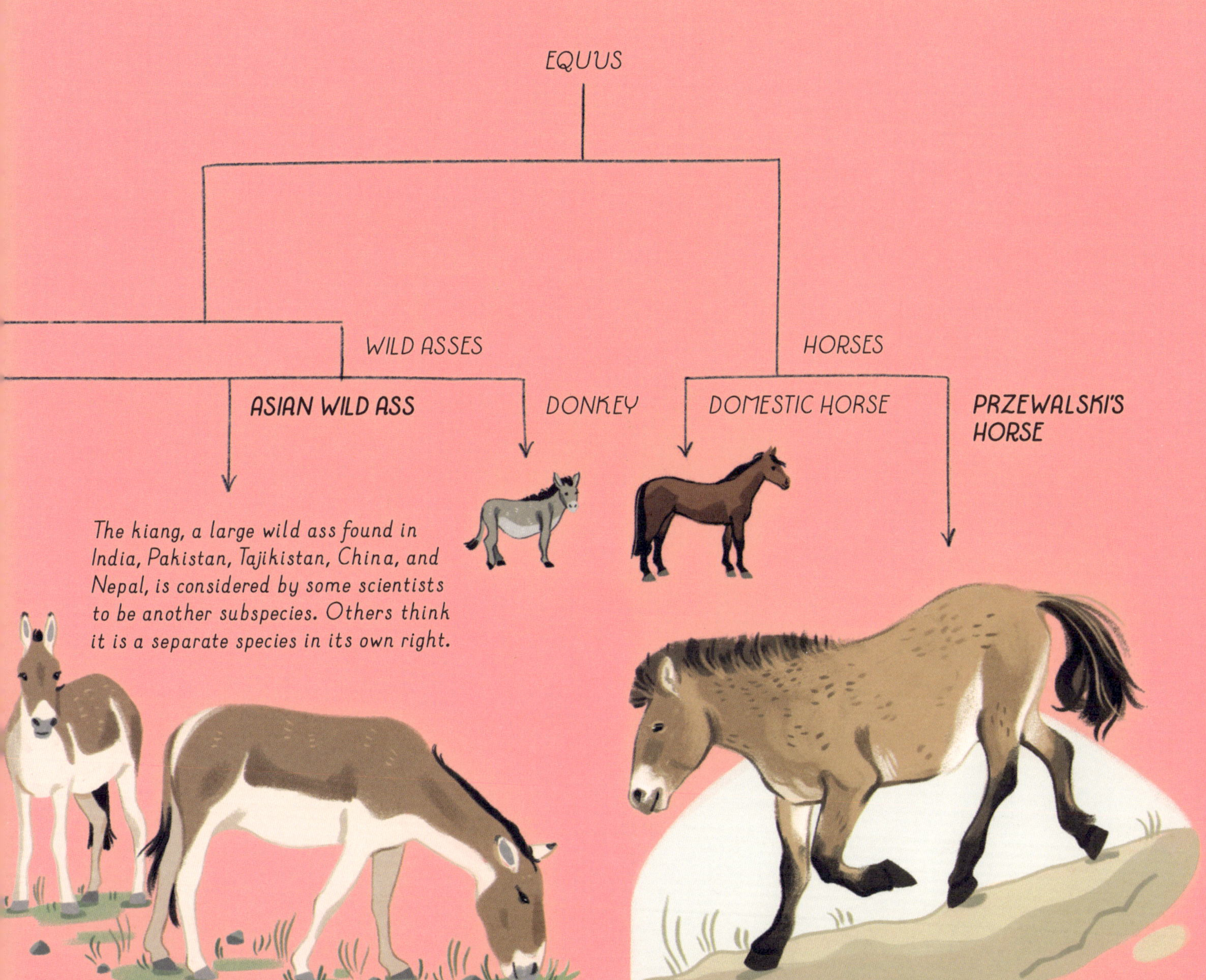

ASIAN WILD ASS

Also known as the onager, the Asian wild ass is made up of four living subspecies: the Turkmenian kulan, Persian onager, Mongolian wild ass, and Indian wild ass. All are endangered due to poaching, drought, and catching diseases from farm animals.

Asian wild asses live in loose family groups and in extreme environments, roaming deserts, steppes, and mountains across Asia. They look more horse-like than their African relatives, with longer legs, larger bodies, and shorter ears. Before donkeys were developed, onagers were tamed in ancient times and trained to pull carts and plows.

PRZEWALSKI'S HORSE

The Przewalski's horse (you say it "sheh-VAHL-skee") is a distant cousin of the domestic horse. With a stocky body and a thick, brush-like mane, Przewalski's are perfectly adapted to a tough life on the windswept steppes and deserts of eastern Asia.

The species was named after a Russian explorer who encountered herds on his travels in the 1870s. Less than 100 years later, the horses were declared extinct in the wild. Breeding programs have reintroduced Przewalski's horses to their original habitats in Mongolia, China, and Russia, but they are still endangered, with only around 2,000 living in the wild today.

1. **ORLOV TROTTER** – RUSSIA
2. **DON** – RUSSIA
3. **VLADIMIR** – RUSSIA
4. **KABARDIN** – RUSSIA
5. **BUDYONNY** – RUSSIA
6. **TERSK** – RUSSIA
7. **ARAB** – BAHRAIN, IRAN, IRAQ, KUWAIT, OMAN, QATAR, SAUDI ARABIA, UAE, YEMEN
8. **CASPIAN** – IRAN
9. **AKHAL-TEKE** – TURKMENISTAN
10. **KARABAKH** – AZERBAIJAN
11. **KARABAIR** – UZBEKISTAN AND TURKMENISTAN
12. **LOKAI** – TAJIKISTAN
13. **MONGOLIAN HORSE** – MONGOLIA AND CHINA
14. **MARWARI** – INDIA
15. **KATHIAWARI** – INDIA
16. **SPITI** – INDIA
17. **SUMBA** – INDONESIA
18. **SANDALWOOD** – INDONESIA
19. **TIMOR** – INDONESIAA
20. **BATAK** – INDONESIA
21. **JAVA** – INDONESIA
22. **KISO** – JAPAN
23. **HOKKAIDO** – JAPAN
24. **TOKARA** – JAPAN

Orlov Trotters have an especially fast trot. Their combination of power and speed made them popular for harness racing in the 19th century.

ASIA

Asia is the original home of the horse. It was here that wild horses were first tamed around 4000 BCE. Ever since, the continent's equines have been shaped by its varied cultures and geography. This is a land of desert-dwelling athletes like the Arab, mighty mountaineers such as the Spiti, and regal Russian trotters. Because they have developed in extreme environments, many Asian breeds are small and stocky equines. But don't let their size fool you. These are some of the toughest ponies around.

THE LAND OF THE HORSE

Horses have been cherished by the people of Mongolia for thousands of years. Many Mongolians are seminomadic, meaning they move from one location to another as the seasons change. Horses are essential to this way of life, acting as the main mode of transportation. In the Mongolian countryside, children learn to ride as young as three years old!

Horses are also used for herding and sport. The country's native breed, the Mongolian Horse, is traditionally ridden by eagle hunters—Kazakh people who use tame golden eagles to hunt in Mongolia's rugged mountains.

A Kabardin puts on fat much more quickly than most other horses. This adaptation originally helped the horse to survive cold Russian winters. If a Kabardin lives in a warmer climate, it needs a lot of daily exercise to make sure it stays a healthy weight.

In Hinduism, Uchchaihshravas is the king of all horses. He has a pure-white coat and seven heads. Uchchaihshravas appears during a struggle between Hindu gods and demons called the Churning of the Milk Ocean.

ORLOV TROTTER

Imagine it is a winter's night in 19th-century Russia and you have been invited to a grand ball. There's only one horse that is strong enough to pull your sleigh over icy roads, battle through blizzards, and get you to the party with speed and style—the Orlov Trotter.

This noble-looking breed was developed by a Russian nobleman, Count Alexei Orlov, in the 1770s by crossing Arab (p.88) stallions with European mares. Throughout the 19th century, Orlov Trotters were used to transport emperors and aristocrats across Russia. The breed declined after the Russian Revolution in 1917, when the royal family's rule came to an end, but Orlov Trotters are still celebrated today as a symbol of the country's culture.

Orlov Trotters are traditionally used in troikas—a type of Russian harness where three horses stand alongside one another to pull a carriage or sleigh. The horse in the middle is the strongest and maintains a steady trot, while the horses on either side canter. Their combined power means a team of horses in a troika can maintain speeds of around 30 miles (50 km) per hour over long distances.

HORSE PROFILE
Country: Russia
Type: Light **Height:** 15.2–17 hands
Colors: Usually gray, but can also be black, bay, or chestnut
Personality: Elegant, fast, hardworking

Orlov Trotters have an especially fast trot. Their combination of power and speed made them popular for harness racing in the 19th century.

DON

This rustic horse is named after the River Don, which flows through the steppes (grasslands) in the south of Russia. Centuries ago, this landscape was home to tough, semi-wild horses. It was also home to a group of people called the Cossacks, like the rider shown here, who were renowned for their horseback riding and battle skills.

The Cossacks mixed the local horses with other Asian breeds to create incredibly hardy equines for their soldiers. In the 19th century, Dons were crossed with Orlov Trotters (see opposite) and Thoroughbreds (p.41) to make the breed larger and more refined. Dons were used by the Russian army up until the 1950s, and today they make robust cross-country and general-riding horses.

HORSE PROFILE

Country: Russia **Type:** Light
Height: 15.1–15.3 hands
Colors: Usually chestnut, but can be bay, black, or gray, too
Personality: Hardy, athletic, even-tempered

VLADIMIR

Russia didn't have its own breed of heavy horse until the early 20th century, when the Vladimir was developed. Farmers in the countryside northeast of Moscow crossed various draft breeds, including Percherons (p.50), Suffolk Punches (p.46), Clydesdales (p.38), and Shires (p.40), to create this strong and reliable horse. It was officially recognized as a breed in 1946.

The Vladimir is an easygoing breed that can help out with all kinds of pulling and carrying jobs on the farm. It also has a very energetic trot, making it well suited for pulling a special type of Russian harness called a troika (see opposite).

HORSE PROFILE

Country: Russia **Type:** Heavy
Height: 15.5–15.8 hands
Colors: Usually bay
Personality: Powerful, energetic, good-tempered

KABARDIN

If you'd like an adventurous outing, take a Kabardin for a ride. For at least 400 years, Kabardins have been bred by tribespeople in the Caucasus Mountains that straddle Russia, Georgia, and Azerbaijan. These horses have exceptionally strong lungs and hearts to cope with the lack of oxygen at high altitudes, and an uncanny ability to pick their way down mountain paths in the darkest of nights and wildest of weathers.

Their ancestors are thought to have been a mix of Turkoman (an old Asian breed), Arab (p.88), and Karabakh (p.90) horses. Historically, farmers grazed herds of Kabardins in high mountain pastures during the summer and brought them down to the foothills for the winter —a tradition that continues today in some rural areas.

Kabardins were used on hill farms for light work, such as pulling hay carts during the harvest, and by armies to cross mountains in times of war. Over the centuries, they have also been used to strengthen other breeds due to their natural hardiness.

HORSE PROFILE
Country: Russia **Type:** Light
Height: 14.1–15.1 hands
Colors: Bay, black, or gray
Personality: Agile, strong, sociable

BUDYONNY

The Budyonny was developed by (and named after) a Russian horse breeder and army commander called Semyon Budyonny between the 1920s and 1940s. Budyonny wanted to create a new breed to boost his country's horse population following World War I (1914–1918) and the Russian Revolution (1917–1923). He crossed Dons (p.85) with Thoroughbreds (p.41) and another Russian breed called a Chernomor—a mountain horse renowned for its stamina and toughness.

Originally used as military riding horses, Budyonnys were bred to be courageous, light on their feet, and smooth to ride. Today, they make great dressage, show jumping, and eventing horses.

HORSE PROFILE

Country: Russia **Type:** Light
Height: 16–16.1 hands
Colors: Typically chestnut, but can be bay, gray, brown, or black
Personality: Energetic, brave, intelligent

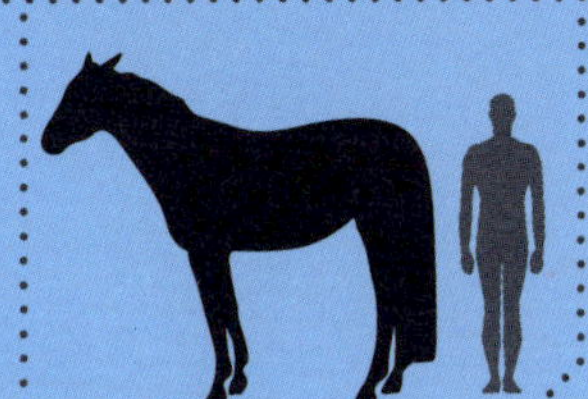

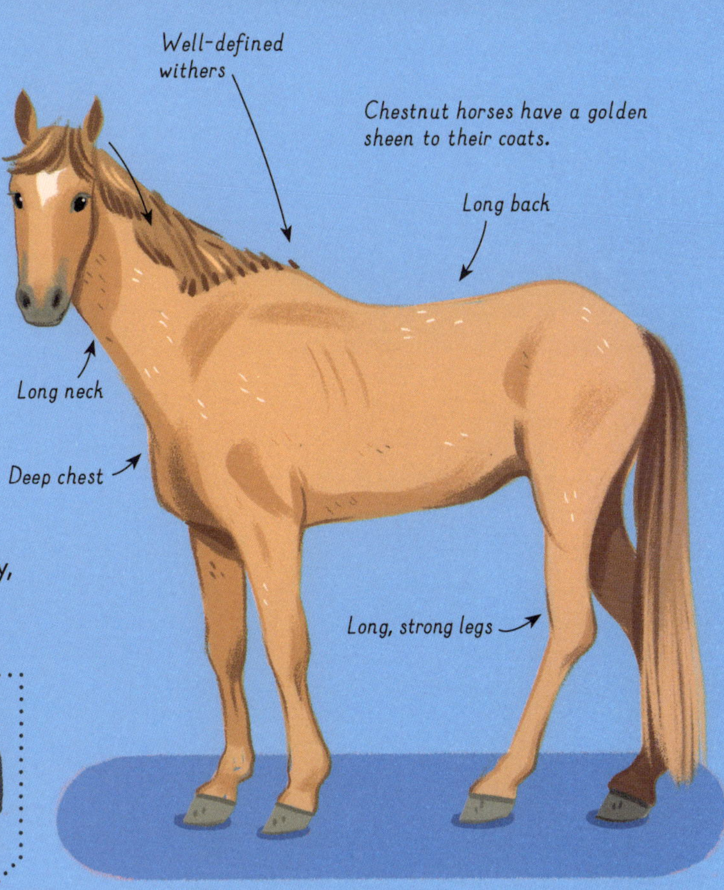

TERSK

Step right up and meet one of the greatest showmen of the horse world. Tersks are born performers and are often ridden by acrobats in Russian circuses, as shown on the left. They are also popular in show jumping, dressage, and eventing.

Like the Budyonny, the Tersk was developed between the 1920s and 1940s in the aftermath of World War I and the Russian Revolution. At a farm in the Caucasus Mountains in the southwest of Russia, Arab horses were mixed with Don (p.85), Kabardin (see opposite), and a now-extinct Ukrainian breed called a Stretlet to make this nimble riding horse.

HORSE PROFILE

Country: Russia **Type:** Light
Height: 15 hands
Colors: Usually gray or white
Personality: Clever, gentle, sure-footed

ARAB

The Arab is one of the world's oldest and most influential breeds. The history of these beautiful horses can be traced to at least 3000 BCE.

They were developed on the Arabian Peninsula by the desert-dwelling Bedouin people as stealthy warhorses. To survive the blistering temperatures and lack of water, Bedouin horses had to be exceptionally tough. The horses lived closely alongside their owners—sometimes sleeping inside their family's tent at night to prevent them from being stolen—so a compact build and gentle disposition was also essential.

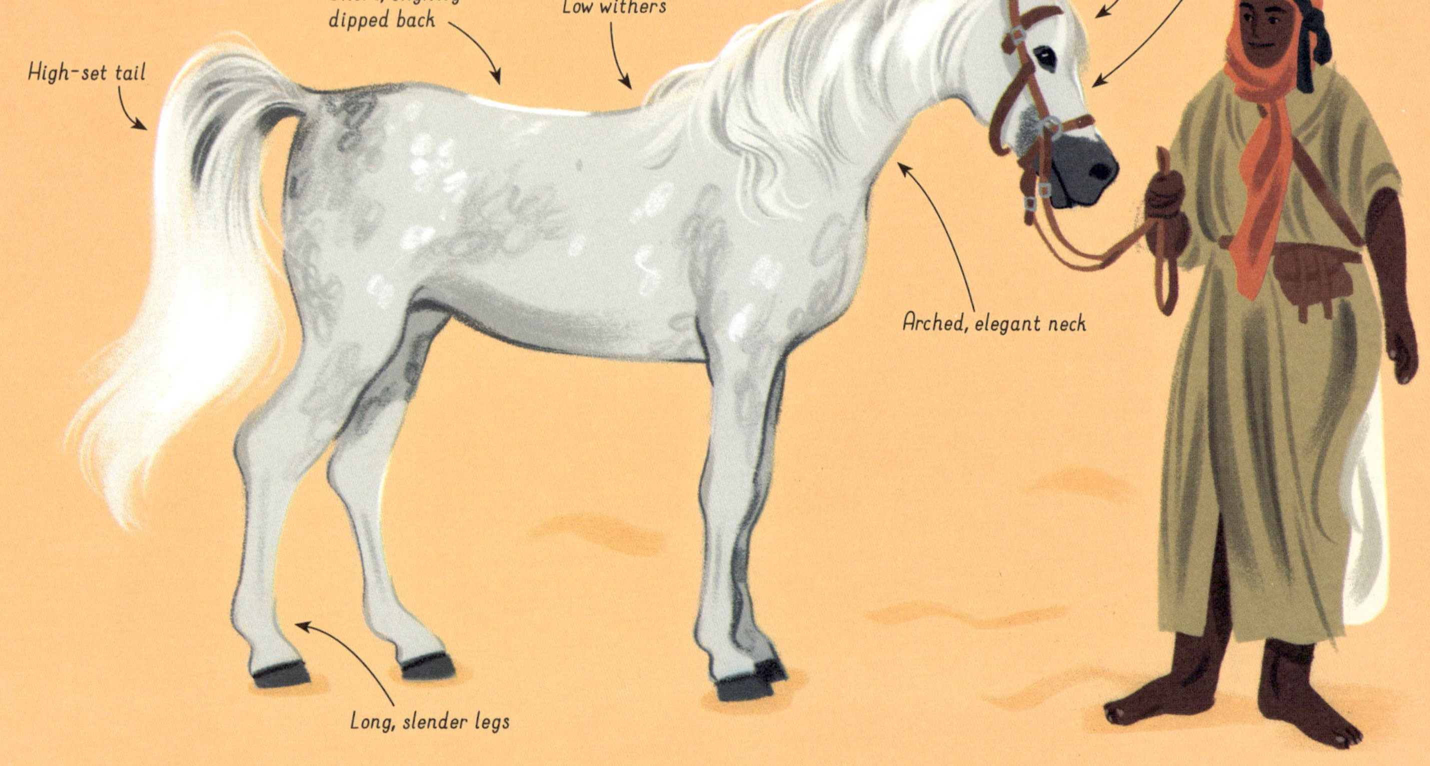

HORSE PROFILE

Country: Bahrain, Iran, Iraq, Kuwait, Oman, Qatar, Saudi Arabia, UAE, and Yemen
Type: Light **Height:** 14.2–15.3 hands
Colors: Bay, gray, chestnut, black, or roan
Personality: Fiery, intelligent, courageous

Arab horses were introduced to Europe from the 8th century onward, and they played a key role in the development of many modern breeds—most famously, the Thoroughbred (p.41). Although they are now found all over the world, Arabs remain true to their desert roots. Combining speed, stamina, agility, and hardiness, they excel in most horsey activities, from show jumping and dressage to endurance racing and ranch work.

CASPIAN

In ancient Persia (c.550–330 BCE), these little horses were kept for chariot racing and as royal pets. But when the Persian Empire ended, its precious horses disappeared . . . or so it seemed. A small population survived in Iran's Alborz Mountains south of the Caspian Sea, where they were used by local people for transportation and carrying goods.

In the 1960s, Louise Firouz, an American living in Iran, came in search of small horses for her horseback riding school. She was struck by the Caspian's story, and devoted the rest of her life to conserving the breed. Caspians make excellent children's horses due to their dainty size, easy movements, and kind characters.

HORSE PROFILE

Country: Iran
Type: Pony **Height:** 11.2–12.2 hands
Colors: All colors except skewbald or piebald
Personality: Gentle, athletic, willing

AKHAL-TEKE

These one-of-a-kind horses come from the Karakum Desert in modern-day Turkmenistan. They were developed at least 3,000 years ago by the nomadic Teke people to carry riders over the vast, dusty landscape. Akhal-Tekes can go for days with little water, run effortlessly across the dunes, and have coats that shimmer like gold in the sun.

Traditionally, these horses spent their days covering long distances in the heat and their nights tethered to their rider's tent. As result, Akhal-Tekes form intense, dog-like bonds with their owners—sometimes even nipping strangers who they see as a threat to their beloved person!

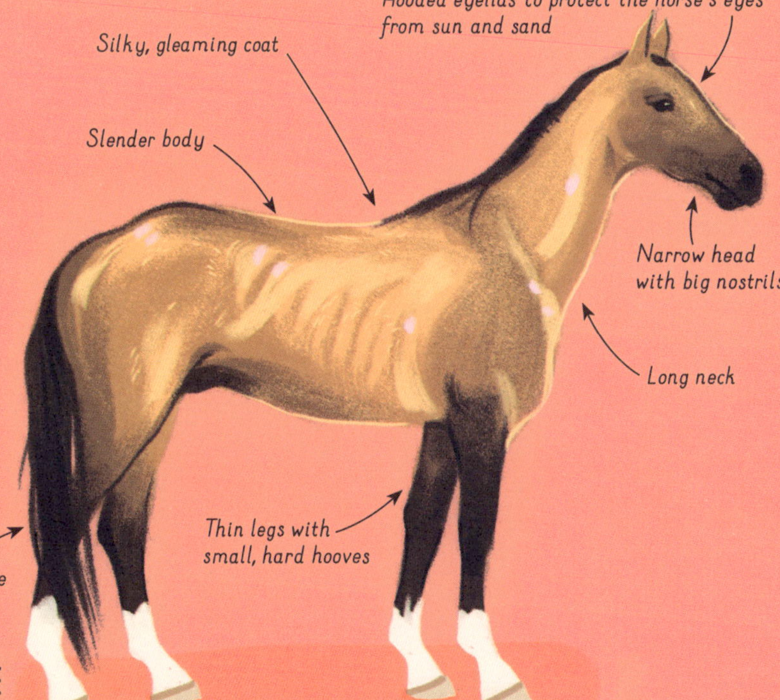

HORSE PROFILE

Country: Turkmenistan
Type: Light **Height:** 14–16 hands
Colors: Often dun, but can be bay, chestnut, black, gray, or silver
Personality: Devoted, intelligent, athletic

An Akhal-Teke's coat hairs have a special structure, which means that sunlight bends as it passes through each individual hair. This gives the horse's coat its magical glimmer.

KARABAKH

The Karabakh is named after a region of Azerbaijan where it has been used as a riding and racing horse for hundreds of years. An adaptable breed, the Karabakh is just as comfortable trotting up treacherous mountain paths as it is galloping across windswept steppes (grasslands).

Although the breed is prized in its homeland and is Azerbaijan's national animal, there are only around 1,000 Karabakhs alive today. These are used in several Azerbaijani horseback riding sports.

HORSE PROFILE
Country: Azerbaijan
Type: Light **Height:** 14–15 hands
Colors: Chestnut, bay, or dun
Personality: Calm, agile, tough

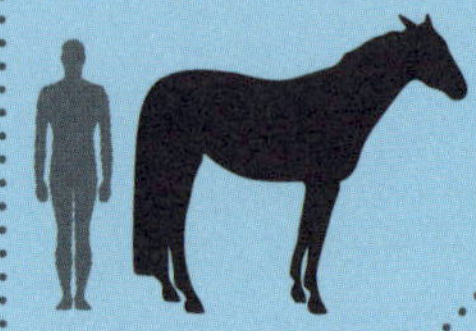

This horse is taking part in the traditional sport of chovgan. A bit like polo, it involves two teams trying to hit a ball into their opponent's goal using wooden mallets.

KARABAIR

One thousand years ago, the area of Central Asia that is now Uzbekistan and Tajikistan sat on ancient trade routes. Desert breeds, such as Arabs (p.88), were sold along these routes and some were eventually crossed with local horses to create the fast and fiery Karabair.

For centuries, this breed has been used to play a dramatic sport called *uloq*, in which teams of riders have to carry a goat carcass to their opponent's goal. In Uzbekistan, the game is played on enormous plains, requiring great stamina and agility from the horses.

HORSE PROFILE
Country: Uzbekistan and Tajikistan
Type: Light **Height:** 14.3–15.2 hands
Colors: Usually bay, chestnut, black, or gray
Personality: Athletic, robust, courageous

LOKAI

The Lokai was developed in the 16th century by tribespeople living in the Pamir Mountains in modern-day Tajikistan. Breeders mixed local horses with various Asian breeds, including Karabairs (see opposite) and Akhal-Tekes (p.89), and later Arabs (p.88), Tersks (p.87), and Thoroughbreds (p.41). The result was a fearless and nimble horse that could carry riders up the steepest of paths.

The Pamirs is a remote landscape of rocky plains, glaciers, and high, snowcapped peaks. With few roads, Lokais are the main means of transportation for people here. These tough horses are also used for *uloq* (see opposite).

HORSE PROFILE

Country: Tajikistan
Type: Light **Height:** 14–15 hands
Colors: Usually bay, gray, or chestnut
Personality: Hardy, sure-footed, loyal

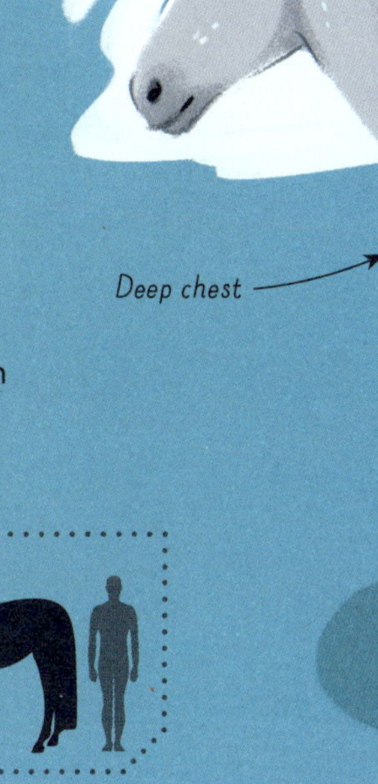

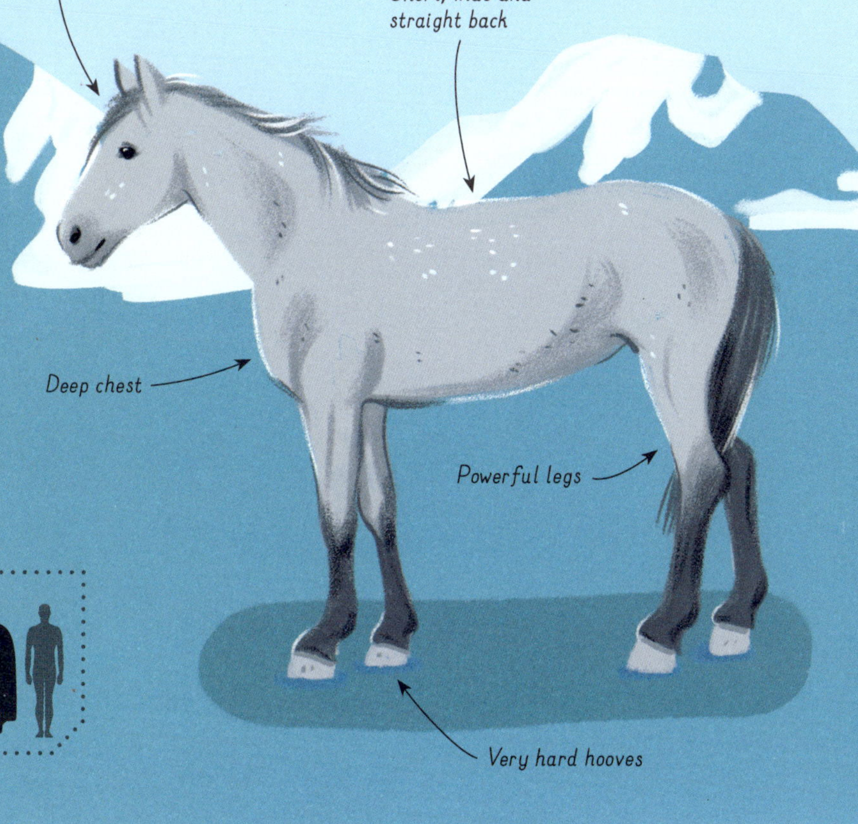

MONGOLIAN HORSE

These immensely hardy horses (despite being pony-size, they are always called horses) have lived semi-wild on the Mongolian steppes for centuries. They stay outside all year round, foraging for their own food and surviving in extreme conditions—temperatures can fall to -40°F (-40°C) in the country during the winter months.

Their ancestors were ridden by the armies of Genghis Khan, the fierce leader of the Mongol Empire, in the 13th century and it's thought the breed has hardly changed since. These horses are still central to the culture of Mongolia's nomadic peoples, who use them for riding, transportation, hunting, and epic long-distance races.

The milk of Mongolian mares is used to produce kumis, a popular drink in Mongolia, while the thick hairs of the horse's tails are used to make rope and violin strings.

HORSE PROFILE

Country: Mongolia and China
Type: Pony **Height:** 12–14 hands
Colors: Various colors, including dun, black, bay, or white
Personality: Independent, powerful, tough

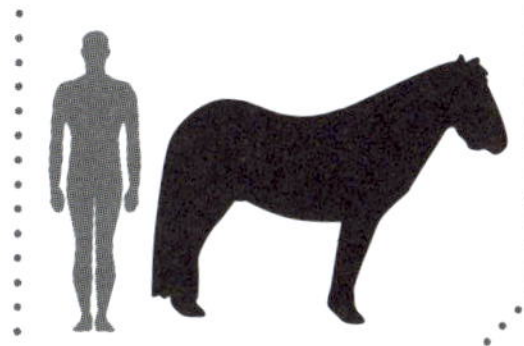

HOW TO SPEAK HORSE

If you haven't spent much time with horses and ponies before, they can seem like intimidating and hard-to-read animals. But they actually send very clear messages with their bodies to tell us how they're feeling. Learning how to read a horse's or pony's body language, and understanding when they're happy, want attention, or need space, means you can have the best possible relationship with your horsey pal.

HORSE HELLOS

Think about how you say hello to another person—you'd usually hug, wave, or maybe shake hands if you don't know them very well. Greetings are just as important to horses. Here's how to say hi to a horse:

- Ask permission from the horse's owner before you approach it. If the owner is happy for you to say hello, walk slowly and confidently toward the horse.

- Always greet a horse from the front where it can see you. Even if you know a horse, you should never approach a horse from behind as they are powerful animals that can kick if they feel frightened.

- Speak softly and calmy—horses prefer low-pitched sounds.

- Study the horse's body language to make sure it's feeling happy and relaxed. Read the rest of this page to learn what to look out for.

- If the horse seems happy, hold out your hand so it can smell you. If a horse is ready for you to stroke it, it will usually lightly touch your hand with its nose. If the horse turns away, it probably doesn't want to be petted right now. Respect this and let it be.

A HAPPY HORSE

A happy horse gives off chilled-out vibes. Its ears are pricked up in an attentive position. Its eyes are open and looking brightly at you. The horse's muzzle looks relaxed and its mouth is closed. A happy horse may be resting one of its back legs by holding its hoof slightly off the ground. It's safe to hold out a hand to see if this horse would like to say hi to you.

A RESTING HORSE

A sleepy horse will look even more relaxed. Its eyes are half-closed, its ears are pointed slightly to the side, and its lower lip may be drooping a little as it dozes. The horse may be resting a back leg and bending its head down. Make sure you approach a sleepy horse carefully (from the front) to avoid startling it.

A WORRIED HORSE

An anxious horse has its ears pointing backward. Its face looks tense, with the muscles above its eyes making a worried V-shape. It may be making a chewing movement with its mouth, too. This sort of behavior suggests the horse is stressed —it may not know you well, so feels uncertain about you approaching. Move away to give this horse some space, so it understands you aren't a threat.

AN UNHAPPY HORSE

An angry or frightened horse makes its feelings clear. Its ears are flattened backward, its teeth are bared, and it's stomping its hooves. This horse is saying, "Back off, or I will bite!" When a horse is this unhappy, you can usually see the whites of its eyes. It may be angrily swishing its tail, sweating and visibly shaking. Stop whatever you're doing and stay away from this horse.

NEIGH-CE TO MEET YOU!

Horses also use sounds to express how they're feeling. There are four types of horsey noises: whinnies (or neighs), nickers, snorts, and squeals. A whinny is a loud, high-pitched neigh. Horses use this sound to call to one another, usually over long distances. A nicker is a low, purring sound. Horses use nickers to say, "Come to me"—for instance, when a mare is calling back her foal, or when a horse sees their favorite human approaching with some tasty hay. Snorts express alarm, while high-pitched squeals are used to communicate aggression.

MARWARI

Once you've met a Marwari you will never forget it—just look at those curly ears! These elegant equines were originally bred as warhorses in the Thar Desert in northwest India from the 12th century.

With a Marwari, a warrior didn't need to worry about getting lost in the dizzying landscape of sand dunes. Marwaris have a heightened sense of smell and hearing, as well as a legendary homing instinct, meaning they'd always get their rider back to camp safely.

By the 1940s, the number of Marwari had fallen, so fans of the breed, including a Maharaja (prince) called Umaid Singhji, established breeding programs to save them. Today, these noble horses are used for weddings and religious festivals in India, as well as for desert horseback riding safaris.

Ears that curve inward so the tips touch

Slim, sleek body with strong back

Slope from croup (rump) to tail

Long legs

Thin skin to cope with hot temperatures in the desert

Very hard hooves

HORSE PROFILE
Country: India
Type: Light **Height:** 14–16 hands
Colors: Various colors, including bay, gray, chestnut, palomino, or skewbald
Personality: Loyal, brave, elegant

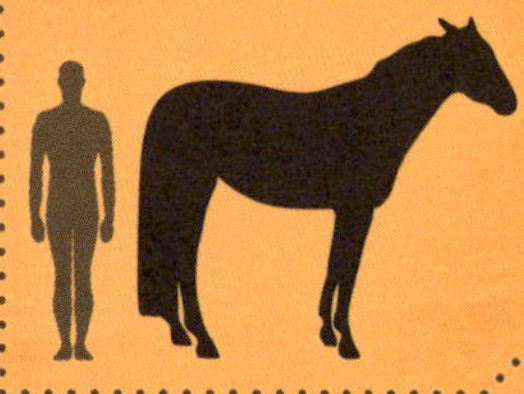

Marwaris have a natural four-beat gait called a revaal or rehwal, which allows the horse to carry its rider smoothly and quickly over tough terrain and long distances.

KATHIAWARI

The Kathiawari is the Marwari's stockier relative. It was developed in the 16th century by Indian royals in the Kathiawar peninsula in west India. They were bred as hardy warhorses, capable of carrying soldiers through the hot desert landscape and able to survive on limited food.

Today, these sensible horses are used for leisure riding and by police forces in India. They are also used for a fast-paced horsey sport called tent-pegging, where a rider uses a sword or lance to pick up a target from the ground while galloping.

HORSE PROFILE
Country: India
Type: Light **Height:** 14–15 hands
Colors: Usually chestnut, but can also be bay, gray, or dun
Personality: Agile, courageous, affectionate

SPITI

The Spiti (also known as the Chamurthi) is only found in a remote valley in the Himalaya Mountains in northern India. Spiti move with ease along icy paths and work comfortably at high altitudes. As a result, they are used for all sorts of jobs, from transporting food and logs to helping farmers carry lambs to meadows in the spring (shown here).

Herds of Spiti are left to roam freely in the valley during summer. Because snow leopards prowl the surrounding slopes, villagers take turns to watch over the ponies and bring them indoors in winter.

HORSE PROFILE
Country: India
Type: Pony **Height:** 9–12 hands
Colors: Various colors, including gray, black, brown, or bay
Personality: Strong, reliable, easygoing

SUMBA

Named after the tropical island of Sumba, this tough, agile pony is thought to be descended from Mongolian and Chinese horses, which were brought to the island by traders and travelers in the 14th century. As well as carrying crops and tourists, the ponies feature in dance festivals on the island, where they wear bells around their legs. Guided by their riders, the ponies move in time to a drumbeat.

HORSE PROFILE
Country: Indonesia
Type: Pony **Height:** 12–12.2 hands
Colors: All solid colors but usually dun
Personality: Tough, athletic, nimble

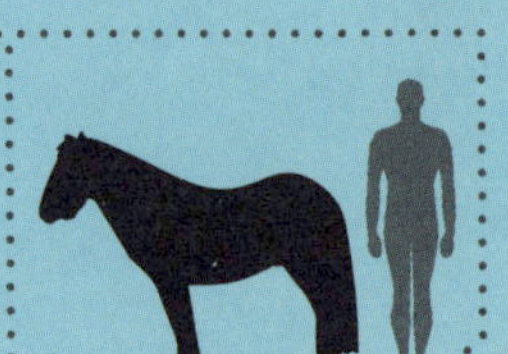

SANDALWOOD

The Sandalwood is named after a fragrant tree that has been an important trade item on Sumba for centuries. The breed was developed from Mongolian and Arab (p.88) horses. Sumba holds a horse festival each year to celebrate this special breed —the ponies wear decorative bridles and compete in riding competitions. The rest of the time, many enjoy swimming in the island's bright blue waters!

HORSE PROFILE
Country: Indonesia
Type: Pony **Height:** 13.1 hands
Colors: Any solid color
Personality: Friendly, fast, tough

TIMOR

Like rough diamonds, these ponies are small, rare, and exceptionally tough. No one is quite sure how long ponies have been on the island of Timor, but it's thought they were introduced by traders from the 6th or 7th century onward. Local people use Timors for racing and farm and cattle work.

HORSE PROFILE

Country: Indonesia
Type: Pony **Height:** 10–12 hands
Colors: Brown, black, bay, or gray
Personality: Strong, hardy, hardworking

BATAK

The hardy Batak was developed by and named after the Batak people who live on the island of Sumatra. They are mainly bred for riding, transporting goods, and racing. Because they are so healthy, Bataks are often used to improve other local breeds as well.

HORSE PROFILE

Country: Indonesia
Type: Pony **Height:** 13 hands
Colors: All solid colors
Personality: Spirited, friendly, strong

JAVA

This pony's ancestors were brought to the tropical island of Java by traders from the 7th century onward. Javas are prized for their hardworking natures. They help farmers collect crops, such as tea and sugar; transport goods and people through the island's cities; and are used for tourist treks to the island's natural wonders.

HORSE PROFILE

Country: Indonesia
Type: Pony **Height:** 11.2–12.2 hands
Colors: Any color
Personality: Hardy, sure-footed, kind-natured

KISO

Japan's famous samurai were powerful warriors and skilled horseback riders who helped rule the country from the 12th to 19th centuries. These fearsome fighters favored one breed in particular—the Kiso. At first glance, these small ponies seem an unusual choice, but they have a brave heart and a noble character to match that of any samurai.

Long before it caught the attention of the samurai, the Kiso was used as a sturdy farm pony in the peaceful forests of the Kiso Valley on Japan's main island, Honshu. Hard-working and gentle, the ponies were treated as part of the family and often lived under the same roof as their owners.

Despite its impressive history, the Kiso almost died out in the 1930s. Although fans set up a conservation project to save the breed, only a few hundred are alive today. You can meet these special ponies at rare-breed centers in Japan, where they are used for trekking and therapy riding.

Thick mane and tail

Round tummy

Short neck

Large head with big, gentle eyes

Strong hooves

Short, sturdy legs

HORSE PROFILE
Country: Japan
Type: Pony **Height:** 13 hands
Colors: Usually bay
Personality: Loyal, strong, kind-natured

Kiso are still used for a traditional samurai sport called yabusame, where a rider on a galloping horse fires arrows at a target.

HOKKAIDO

Hokkaido ponies (also known as Dosanko) come from the mountainous island of Hokkaido in the far north of Japan. In the 15th century, fisherman from Honshu took horses to the island each spring to help them haul cartloads of herring during the fish harvest.

HORSE PROFILE
Country: Japan
Type: Pony **Height:** 13–13.2 hands
Colors: Various colors but often roan
Personality: Resourceful, strong, gentle

At the end of the season, the horses were left behind to fend for themselves and they developed into a strong and resourceful breed. In the past, the ponies were used for farmwork and transporting goods. Today, you're more likely to see them carrying tourists or pulling sleds through the island's snowy mountains.

TOKARA

This extremely rare pony comes from a group of remote islands in the south of Japan. Little was known about the Tokara until the 1950s, when a Japanese professor traveled to the islands and encountered a herd.

It's thought the ancestors of these hardy ponies were brought to the islands in the late 19th century and used by local people for transportation and to work on sugarcane farms. Today, the Tokara is celebrated as a "natural monument," reflecting its important role in the region's farming history.

Strong neck
Delicate head
Thick mane and tail
Round body
Short legs
Hard hooves

HORSE PROFILE
Country: Japan
Type: Pony **Height:** Around 12 hands
Colors: Usually black or seal brown
Personality: Tough, independent, gentle

WARHORSES

From carrying soldiers into the heart of battle to pulling equipment and delivering medical supplies, millions of horses, ponies, mules, and donkeys have played important roles in wars throughout history. Without the help of these faithful and courageous animals, many battles could not have been fought or won.

SADDLE UP

People didn't start riding horses into battle until around 800–900 BCE. This transformed the way people fought one another—a group of soldiers on horseback (called cavalry) was quicker and more powerful than a group of soldiers on foot.

The invention of the stirrup in China in around 300 CE gave soldiers greater stability in the saddle and allowed them to control their horses more easily on the battlefield.

An ancient people called the Scythians (you say it "Sih-thee-uns") from Central Asia were some of the first people to use horses in battle (above). It's possible these fearsome fighters inspired the ancient Greek myth of the centaur (left), a creature that is part human, part horse.

CALL IN THE CAVALRY

In the medieval era (400–1400 CE), horses were essential to armies all over the world. Muslim soldiers in Asia and Africa used light horses to carry them swiftly into battle. In Europe, knights favored heavy horses that could support the weight of their steel armor. However, the development of guns from the 14th century onward meant that European armies stopped wearing heavy armor and switched to using faster, more agile breeds.

HORSES IN WORLD WAR I

Millions of horses and ponies took part in World War 1 (1914–1918), one of the biggest conflicts in human history. Many were civilian horses that had been bought by armies from farms, families, businesses, and racing stables. Here are some of the ways these brave equines supported soldiers:

Cavalry – at the start of the war, thousands of troops on horseback were sent to the front lines.

Ambulances – one of the most important jobs was pulling ambulance wagons. When roads had been destroyed or the terrain was so treacherous that motor vehicles couldn't get through, horses were vital for rescuing injured soldiers and delivering medical aid.

Transportation and heavy lifting – horses, donkeys, mules, and ponies were used throughout the war to carry ammunition, haul equipment, and deliver supplies.

CARING FOR WARHORSES

Without horses, armies on both sides wouldn't have been able to function, so special hospitals were set up to treat and care for injured horses. Even so, the front line would have been a terrifying place for these animals. It is estimated that 8 million horses, ponies, mules, and donkeys died from disease and injuries during World War I.

A special type of gas mask was developed for horses serving in the trenches to help protect them from poisonous gas attacks.

WARRIOR'S STORY

The life of a Thoroughbred called Warrior tells the story of millions of horses who served in World War I. Before the war, Warrior lived a peaceful life in the UK. He accompanied his owner, General Jack Seely, to the battlefront in 1914. Warrior carried Jack into some of the deadliest battles of the war, faced attacks from machine guns, and survived being buried in mud and trapped in burning stables. Remarkably, both Warrior and Jack survived the war and returned home in 1918.

In 2014, Warrior was posthumously awarded the Dickin Medal, the highest award any animal can receive for bravery, in recognition of all animals that served in World War I.

No one knows for sure how Brumby horses got their name. One theory is that some of the first of the horses to roam freely in Australia belonged to a soldier and farrier (an expert in hoof care) called James Brumby.
BRUMBY
AUSTRALIA
AUSTRALIAN PONY
AUSTRALIA
AUSTRALIAN DRAFT
AUSTRALIA
AUSTRALIAN STOCK HORSE
AUSTRALIA
Australian Drafts have been bred to have little or no white markings on them. This is because pink skin (which sits under white fur) can burn more easily in the hot Australian sun.

AUSTRALIA AND NEW ZEALAND

There were no horses in Australia until the 18th century, when they were introduced by European colonizers. Similarly, the first horses to land in New Zealand set hoof on its islands in the early 19th century. These early horses were eventually used to create three Aussie all-rounders—a trusty riding pony, an agile light horse, and a mighty heavy horse. A small population of horses also escaped into the Australian wilderness and New Zealand mountains, evolving into two unique feral breeds. If you need a tough friend to gallop through the Outback or a trusty pony to carry you stylishly around the show ring, you'll find them in this chapter.

Feral brumbies, shown here running free in the Australian countryside, have a problematic reputation. For many Indigenous Australians, the Brumby is a reminder of a time when European settlers arrived in the country and took Indigenous land. Large herds of free-roaming Brumbies can also damage wild habitats.

KAIMANAWA HORSE
NEW ZEALAND

MĀORI HORSES

The Māori people of Aotearoa (New Zealand) first encountered horses in 1814, when British colonizers introduced the animals to the country. Horses were sometimes presented as gifts to Māori chiefs by settlers. As the number of horses grew, tribes started to buy their own. This established a rich tradition of Māori horsemanship that continues to this day.

AUSTRALIAN PONY

This dainty breed from Down Under has a fun, friendly character that reflects its Aussie heritage. The country's only pony breed, the Australian Pony was developed during the 19th century using breeds from Europe and Asia. These included Welsh Ponies (p.42), Exmoors (p.57), Thoroughbreds (p.41), Hungarian Ponies, and Timors (p.97).

The Australian Pony has inherited the best traits of its ancestors and is very popular in its home country. It's an adaptable and robust breed that can be counted on to carry its rider over tough terrain in hot weather as well as proudly compete in the show ring. Australian Ponies can be used for all sorts of horsey activities, including dressage, driving competitions, and gymkhanas.

These pretty ponies love to be groomed and made a fuss of, and make wonderful first ponies for children due to their affectionate natures—bring on the cuddles!

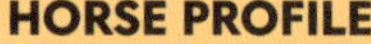

HORSE PROFILE
Country: Australia
Type: Pony **Height:** 11–14 hands
Colors: Usually gray, but can be any solid color
Personality: Affectionate, enthusiastic, reliable

AUSTRALIAN STOCK HORSE

The first horses to arrive in Australia were a mix of breeds, including Thoroughbreds (p.41) and Spanish horses. Only the toughest survived the long voyage and, when they arrived, the challenging climate in their new home.

Over time, these horses were bred together to create a distinct type of light working horse. These horses were used on cattle ranches and as warhorses, prized for their agility and endurance. This handsome breed was officially recognized and named the Australian Stock Horse in 1971.

HORSE PROFILE
Country: Australia
Type: Light **Height:** 15–16.2 hands
Colors: All solid colors
Personality: Hardy, adaptable, surefooted

AUSTRALIAN DRAFT

Many of the early European settlers in Australia were farmers, who traveled to the continent with their heavy horses in tow. Four breeds were particularly popular—Shires (p.40), Clydesdales (p.38), Suffolk Punches (p.46), and Percherons (p.50). These breeds were mixed together to create the Australian Draft.

HORSE PROFILE
Country: Australia
Type: Heavy **Height:** 16–17.2 hands
Colors: All solid colors
Personality: Strong, intelligent, sweet-natured

Reliable and kindhearted, Australian Drafts were used to plow the land and pull wagons into town. A few small farms still use Australian Drafts, but most are bred today for horse shows or, sometimes, forestry work.

BRUMBY

In the 19th century, European settlers flocked to Australia. Many came to mine the land for gold or build farms. Horses were essential companions—they carried people across the wild parts of the country called the Outback and hauled goods and equipment. But when farms failed or the gold ran out, the horses were often abandoned.

These horses became survival experts, thriving in habitats across the country—from harsh scrubland to remote mountain forests—and outwitting hunters who tried to capture them in attempts to control the number of feral horses. They came to be known as Brumbies and around 400,000 roam Australia today.

While some Australians celebrate these horses as an Australian breed, others see Brumbies as a problem. Because the horses have no natural predators, large herds can cause damage to the country's wild habitats. Various charities advocate for the humane control of Brumby numbers and run sanctuaries to care for them.

Straight head with big, intelligent eyes

Elegant neck

Short back

Very strong hooves

Slim but strong legs

HORSE PROFILE

Country: Australia **Type**: Light
Height: Varies but usually around 15 hands
Colors: All colors
Personality: Tough, intelligent, independent

Brumbies are free-spirited equines, but they can be tamed. They are so at home in Australia's wild landscapes that they make excellent trail-riding horses.

KAIMANAWA HORSE

There were no horses in New Zealand until 1814, when a stallion and two mares arrived with British settlers. Early settlers used horses for farming and transportation, and also presented them as gifts to the country's Indigenous Māori people.

By 1876, a herd of various breeds was spotted living wild in the Kaimanawa Mountains, a landscape of tussocky grasslands and jagged peaks on the country's North Island. It's thought these horses had been let loose by their European or Māori owners or escaped from sheep farms. Over time, they bred together to create a totally unique type of feral horse—the Kaimanawa.

Each year, these hardy horses are rounded up and around 200 are removed from the herd to be rehomed. This is done to control the number of horses living on the mountains, where endangered plants are found. When tamed, Kaimanawas can be trained for various events, such as show jumping and endurance, and make exceptionally loyal riding buddies.

HORSE PROFILE
Country: New Zealand **Type:** Light
Height: Usually around 15 hands (but can be as small as 12 hands or as tall as 16 hands)
Colors: Any coat color
Personality: Tough, intelligent, intrepid

RECORD-BREAKING HORSES

As a horsey mega-fan you don't need to be told that horses are incredible animals—but do you know just how amazing they are? Read on to learn some astounding facts about our equine friends.

GENTLE GIANT

A Shire Horse named Sampson, from Bedfordshire, UK, was the tallest horse ever recorded. In 1850, he measured 21.25 hands (7 ft. 2.5 in., or 2.19 m) high. Sampson was a giant even by Shire Horse standards—most male Shires are around 17 hands high. His owner believed Sampson was so tall thanks to his diet of oats and barley.

OLD BILLY

The title of "oldest horse that ever lived" goes to Old Billy. Billy was a mixed breed (possibly a Cob and Shire Horse cross) who spent most of his life tugging barges along canals in central England. He was born in 1760 and died in 1822 at the grand old age of 62.

TINY BUT TOUGH

The smallest horse ever recorded was a miniature brown mare called Thumbelina, from Missouri, USA. Little Thumbelina was just 4.2 hands (17.5 in., or 44.5 cm) tall—roughly as big as an English bulldog. She may have been small, but Thumbelina had a big personality. Apparently, she thought nothing of escaping under fences and bossing around other, much bigger horses on her farm!

THE MANE EVENT

An American Paint Horse called JJS Summer Breeze holds the record for "longest tail on a horse." This horsey Rapunzel's long locks measure 12 ft. 6 in. (381 cm). It takes her owner three hours to shampoo and brush Summer's tremendous tail.

SUPER SPEED

The speediest horse is a Thoroughbred called Winning Brew. She smashed horsey records in 2008 by reaching speeds of 43.97 miles (70.76 km) per hour in a two-furlong (1,320 ft./402 m) race held in the USA.

HIGH JUMPS

The highest jump ever recorded was 8 ft. 1.25 in. (2.47 m) tall. It was jumped by a horse called Huaso ex-Faithful, in Santiago, Chile, on February 5, 1949. The highest jump by a miniature horse was 3 ft. 10 in. (1.17 m). This record was set in Bargemon, France, on May 2, 2020, by a miniature horse called Zephyr (shown here).

EQUINE EINSTEIN

A horse that can do math?! A super-smart rescue horse called Lukas holds the record for the "most numbers correctly identified by a horse in one minute." Clever Lukas can identify 19 numbers (with his nose).

GLOSSARY

Breeding program
The planned breeding of a group of animals. This helps to establish breeds that share similar characteristics or features.

Bridle
A set of straps put around a horse's head to help a rider control the horse's movements.

Canter
A three-beat gait. This means that the horse's feet move in a special pattern to create three beats: first one of the back feet moves (1st beat), then two diagonal feet move at the same time (2nd beat), and then the final front foot moves (3rd beat). A canter is faster than a trot, but slower than a gallop.

Colt
A young male horse, usually less than four years old.

Dickin Medal
A British medal awarded to an animal that has performed an act of great heroism.

Domestication
The process of taming a wild animal.

Double coat
A coat formed of two layers—a rough, weather-resistant topcoat and a soft, thick undercoat.

Dressage
A horse sport where a horse and its rider perform a series of particular movements, sometimes accompanied by music.

Driving
In general terms, when a horse, pony, donkey, or mule pulls a cart or wagon. Driving is also a type of horse sport where a horse, or team of horses, pulls a two- or four-wheeled carriage.

Endangered
Refers to an animal that is at risk of disappearing forever from the wild forever.

Endurance riding
A horse sport where horses and their riders race outdoors over long distances.

Equine
A member of the horse family, or relating to horses.

Eventing
A horse sport where a horse and its rider compete across three events—cross-country, dressage, and show jumping.

Farrier
A person who specializes in horse hoof care, including fitting horseshoes and trimming hooves.

Feathering
Long hairs that grow around the hooves of some breeds of horses and ponies, such as Clydesdales.

Flaxen
A pale-yellow color.

Foal
A baby horse.

Furlong
An old-fashioned imperial unit of distance equivalent to around 220 yards (201 meters). The term is still used in horse racing.

Gait
The pattern of leg movement that horses use to get around. Most horses have four natural gaits: walk, trot, canter, and gallop. Some breeds, such as the Peruvian Paso and the Missouri Fox Trotter, have been bred to have special gaits.

Gallop
A fast, four-beat gait (meaning each foot moves independently). A full-on run.

Gymkhana
An event, usually for children, involving horseback riding and jumping competitions.

Hand
An old-fashioned unit of measurement, which is still used today to measure horses. One hand is equal to 4 inches (10.16 cm). A horse's height is measured from the ground to its withers (the highest part of a horse's back).

Heavy horse
Large, strongly built breeds that have been bred to pull heavy loads. They are also known as draft horses. Examples of heavy breeds include the Shire, Percheron, and Italian Heavy Draft.

Light horse
Slender breeds that have been bred mainly for riding and horse sport. Examples of light breeds include the Thoroughbred, Quarter Horse, and Andalusian.

Mare
A female horse.

Mottle
A speckled pattern on a horse's coat.

Mount
A horse that you ride.

Pace
A two-beat gait. In the pace, the two feet on the same side of the horse move forward at the same time. Compare with a trot.

Packhorse
A horse (or pony, donkey, or mule) used to carry loads on its back.

Pony
A small, stocky type of horse, usually below 14.2 hands high at the withers.

Ranch
A very large farm, typically in North America, South America, and Australia, where horses (or other animals such as cows and sheep) are kept.

Savanna
A flat area of grassland, with few trees, usually found in tropical parts of the world.

Stallion
A male horse.

Steed
A horse that you ride.

Steppe
A large, flat area of dry grassland, typically in eastern Europe and Central Asia.

Stirrup
A metal frame or hoop that is attached to the saddle by a strap, for holding the rider's foot.

Stud farm
A farm where horses and ponies are bred.

Trail riding
Riding on off-road paths.

Trot
A two-beat gait where the two feet diagonally opposite each other move forward at the same time (compare to a pace). A trot is faster than a walk but slower than a canter.

Warmblood
An athletic type of horse, bred for sport, which often has Arab or Thoroughbred ancestry, plus some "coldblood" heritage. *Coldblood* is another word for a heavy or draft horse.

Weaning
The process by which an animal stops being dependent on its mother's milk and starts eating solid food.

Withers
The highest part of a horse's back—from where a horse's height is measured.

Yearling
A young horse that is a year old.

INDEX